Catholicism at the Crossroads

CATHOLICISM AT THE CROSSROADS

How the Laity
Can Save the Church

PAUL LAKELAND

continuum

NEW YORK • LONDON

2007
The Continuum International Publishing Group Inc
80 Maiden Lane, New York, New York 10038

The Continuum International Publishing Group Ltd
The Tower Building, 11 York Road, London SE1 7NX

Continuum is a member of Green Press Initiative, a nonprofit program dedicated to supporting publishers in their efforts to reduce their use of fiber obtained from endangered forests. For more information, go to www.greenpressinitiative.org.

Printed in the United States of America

Library of Congress Cataloging-in-Publication Data

Lakeland, Paul, 1946-
    Catholicism at the crossroads : how the laity can save the church / Paul Lakeland.
        p. cm.
    Includes bibliographical references and index.
    ISBN-13: 978-0-8264-2810-3 (pbk. : alk. paper)
    ISBN-10: 0-8264-2810-X (pbk. : alk. paper)
    1. Lay ministry—Catholic Church. 2. Laity. 3. Catholic Church. I. Title.

BX1920.L35 2007
262'.152—dc22

                                                    2007003482

This book is dedicated to the wonderful people
of Voice of the Faithful, FutureChurch,
and Call to Action, in recognition
of their boundless love and concern
for our church.

Contents

℘

PREFACE

In the years since my book on the church, *The Liberation of the Laity* (2003), I have traveled all over the country speaking to groups of Catholics eager to find answers to their questions and ways to remain hopeful about the church. I have been inspired by their energy and example, and I have tried to offer them what help I can from a theologian's perspective. But I have come to realize that much of what I wrote in that earlier book is not expressed in ways that are always helpful. So in what follows I am talking to Catholics in language that requires no special expertise in theology and that will not necessitate constant reference to a dictionary. The book, I hope, also reflects the fact that, four years on, my thinking has developed and—perhaps—deepened.

This book is written for adult Catholics who want an adult church that can sustain their adult faith. The chapters that follow will address a series of questions that bother such people. But it is also written in the knowledge that not all adult Catholics are ready, willing, and able to plunge into the complexities of academic theology. While this book will have some amount of explication of events, of history, and even theology within it, its primary purpose is practical. If it is successful, lay Catholics and others will be able to use it, alone or in groups, to energize themselves in the fight to keep the church faithful to Vatican II. It is not a book about Vatican II, but a book about how to be church in the spirit of the council. In the end, I believe, it is a work that sets out to reassure liberal Catholics that their position on issues is perfectly justifiable and that their vision of the church as an open and progressive community is at least as orthodox as the more conservative models that seem currently to be in the ascendancy. We need to be able to feel good about ourselves and good about our church. We need to be able to look optimistically on what our church can do for the world. We need to be able to be proud of the American Catholic Church, not only for what it has done and not only for the many wonderful people whose selfless work contributes to its vitality in so many ways but also for the public and even institutional face it presents to the wider world.

Because I intend this work as a teaching tool addressed to an audience that is not trained in academic theology, I have avoided the distraction of footnotes. But because I am also very much aware that many Catholic laypeople and not a few priests like to look more deeply into this or that matter, at the end of each chapter I have provided some brief annotated bibliographical aids and some questions that might be used as a basis for discussion.

Two chapters of this book have appeared previously in whole or in part in other publications. I am grateful for permission to reprint the bulk of chapter 5, which previously appeared in *Church Ethics and Its Organizational Context: Learning from the Sex Abuse Scandal in the Catholic Church,* edited by Jean M. Bartunek, Mary Ann Hinsdale, and James F. Keenan (Lanham, Md.: Rowman & Littlefield, 2006), and portions of chapter 3, originally published as "Accountability, Credibility and Authority," *New Theology Review* 19, no. 1 (February 2006).

As always, I have many people to thank for making it possible for me to complete this book and put it before you. Frank Oveis of Continuum Press is first among these. I have known him to be special since the day I saw him standing out in the rain on a wintry Saturday in New Haven at 9:00 in the morning, handing out fliers for one of my books to people arriving at a theological conference. His generosity and enthusiasm, blended with his incomparable depth of experience in religious publishing, make him the perfect publisher, this time as last time, and someone you would be proud to call a friend. My colleagues at Fairfield University come next, in particular the critical voice of my good friend John Thiel, who reads my work gently but thoroughly with the skills of the great theologian that he is—and that I could only dream about being. I am thankful too for Fairfield University's gift of an endowed chair, which in the last two years has provided me with a little more time to write. For the first time in the career of a harried undergraduate college professor

I have produced a book that was not written during a sabbatical leave. In the wider theological community I am most appreciative of the wonderful ecumenical solidarity and genuine friendship that I have found in the Nashville-based Workgroup for Constructive Theology over the last seven years or so, which has helped me not to become bogged down in the troubles of the church, an occupational hazard for an ecclesiologist. I have also benefited enormously from the advice of Anne Dennean, John Santa, and John Tyminski, who subjected the manuscript to a careful reading informed by their deep knowledge of the working church. As always, I thank my wife, Beth Palmer, and my son, Jonathan, for the space to do what I do and the distractions that are needed to put it all in perspective.

This book is dedicated to all the wonderful Catholic laypeople I have met around the country in the last three years who are struggling in hope for the future of a church that they love deeply, often in very difficult situations. Whether they belong to Voice of the Faithful or Call to Action or FutureChurch or simply their local parish, I salute them all. And I hope that this book may be of some small service in pursuing the rescue of our church from its present perilous situation.

Introduction

STEPPING UP
TO THE PLATE

We American Catholics live in a church that isn't working very well, and it is up to us to do something about it. Around the world, the church has different challenges in different places, most of them to do with local history and culture. There are some universal issues, but even those are affected by local considerations. Here in the United States we have our own particular vices and weaknesses, and they affect the church in ways not dissimilar from those in which they have an impact on society at large. But we also have our own virtues and strengths, which can be brought to bear on the problems of the church. American history, American values, American traditions at their best have much to offer the worldwide Catholic Church, but most immediately they may suggest paths for our communities of faith here at home. Of course, we have much to gain also from what other cultures and other peoples can teach us. But this book is principally about the American Catholic Church, about what is right with it and what is wrong with it and about how we can draw on our cultural resources to work to put right the things that are not. This is our contribution, as humble as it may be, to saving the church. Nothing less is at stake than the future shape of the American Catholic Church.

The principal theme of this book is the need for "an open church in an open society." A commitment to an open society, at least in principle, is fundamental to American culture and the American political tradition. We could have said "a democratic church in a democratic society," but this can be misleading. For one thing, Americans tend to think that the be-all and end-all of democracy is the vote. Of course it is important, at least as a symbol. But democracy neither begins nor ends with the vote. A democratic society and a democratic church require public participation in the debates through which decisions are made about law, public policy, and even the values that we propose to uphold. The public forum that we need to make these debates possible requires openness, both to sources of information and to the ideas that will be offered from all sectors of the community. We cannot have a society or a church that respects the freedom of its members without a commitment to openness.

By calling for an open church in an open society, we are also pointing to the fact that there are interconnections between the two. Any national church is influenced by its national culture, of course, but the hope for Christians is also that the society will be open to the influence of Christian voices. In our American society today there are dangerously undemocratic currents at work, seeming to make a mockery of the American commitment to an open society. The principle isn't matched by the practice. Our freedoms are undoubtedly limited by the role of money in the political process, by the unchecked use of corporate political lobbying, by unholy wars justified by lies and misinformation in the cause of the so-called war on terror, by cavalier disregard for international law and human rights, and by the clandestine affronts to our personal liberties undertaken by the executive branch of government without judicial or congressional oversight. Our Catholic Church is also deeply compromised in its commitment to the freedom of the children of God, most particularly by its exclusion of the overwhelming majority of Catholics from any role in leadership or the formation of teaching, and by the ways in which it continues to discriminate against women. As a consequence of these currents in church and society, the church cannot speak clearly to American society on issues of freedom; our Catholic praxis of internal restraints on freedom makes it much more difficult to engage the attention of the American public in general, even when we have something worthwhile to say.

The common factor between church and society is that all adult Catholics act in both realms. The difference is that Catholics take for granted in their secular lives certain freedoms that they cannot find in their church, for example, the exercise of the vote, a free press, and official channels through which leadership can hear from the masses. The consequence of this disparity is that we must either find a way to justify the special rules that seem to apply in the church or we must recognize that the church is at fault in not recognizing the legitimate freedoms of the people. It cannot work both ways. We are either a legitimately clericalist community, in which the will of God or the intentions of Jesus or the power of the Spirit works to maintain a situation in which only celibate men have the opportunities to lead, or we are a dysfunctional community marked by the infantilization of the laity. In the latter case, it must surely be the will of God, the design of Jesus, and the work of the Spirit that we try to overcome the barriers to the freedom in Christ proclaimed in the New Testament. Which option we choose will depend in large part on what we think the phrase "freedom in Christ" actually means.

There will probably always be a Roman Catholic Church, but it may not always be worthy of the name. Christ's promise that the Spirit will be with the church forever means that, in the long run, the church will succeed in being the sacrament of God's loving presence in the world. In the long run, the church will persevere in truth. But the promise of the Spirit does not mean that in the near or middle distance the church will always and everywhere be faithful to its mission. There have been times in the church's history when it has clearly gone off the rails. There have been teachings that, however understandable their historical origins might have been, have long outlived their usefulness by the time the church finds the way to say that what it once taught is in fact against the spirit of the gospel. So, the Catholic Church that promoted the Crusades or that was led by the corrupt papacy of the late Middle Ages, the Catholic Church that burned heretics and condemned Galileo, the Catholic Church that defended slavery long after it could reasonably be defended was a church in error. In error, it was not in the Spirit. The Spirit returned to it in and through the prayer and faithful struggles of Catholics, who were often persecuted by the very church they sought to reclaim.

In the early years of the twenty-first century we are once again in a period in which the future of the church rests in the hands and hearts of ordinary Catholics. Today, many of our bishops and not a few of the lay members of the church are attracted to a dangerously incomplete vision of Catholicism. The version of Catholicism that they are strenuously promoting is one that sidesteps the major themes and key insights of Vatican II. The fundamentals of faith are no different now from what they were in the years before the council, and there is much to commend in the church of the past, much with which we must remain in continuity. But we live in the era of Vatican II, bound to faithfulness to the developing insights about Catholicism that the bishops brought to expression in the event of the council and in the sixteen documents that they approved. If the reiteration of unchanging truth is the bedrock faith of the council documents, the developing and even new emphases of the council represent the imagined shape of the church. In the last two or three decades, that effort to reshape the church has been smothered by a campaign of misrepresentation, an effort to blunt the voice of the Spirit. It has happened all over the world, and the United States has not escaped the damage. Today we have no option but to take up the challenge of faithfulness. Ordinary Catholics will have to strive for post–Vatican II orthodoxy if our leaders are not going to do so. And let us be careful to defend the word "orthodoxy" from those who would steal it away from us. "Orthodox" does not mean "conservative" or "traditionalist," and "liberal" does not mean "heterodox." Orthodoxy is a spectrum bounded by the gospel, not an ideology pronounced by an institution or promoted by some of its bishops. Orthodoxy is roomy enough for most liberals and most conservatives.

The encouragement to ordinary Catholics to see the church's faithfulness to the gospel as their responsibility comes from Vatican

II itself. Perhaps, moved by the Spirit, the council fathers had a premonition of the backlash that so much of their thinking would inspire, and it was this that led them so forcibly to assert the importance of lay involvement in the life of the church. Vatican II rediscovered the sacrament of baptism for the institutional church, making clear that it is far more than a mere initiation into the community. It is the assumption of a priestly responsibility. It is the foundation of the mission of all Christians. It is the basis for the fundamental equality of all and for the shared responsibility that comes with that status. For many centuries an unbalanced attention to the importance of the ordained priesthood had obliterated any attention to the baptismal priesthood. That we the church are a priestly people was at best an empty truism, at worst just forgotten, in the urge to assert and defend the powers of orders and jurisdiction that were vested in the ordained ministry of priests and bishops.

Vatican II changed everything for ordinary Catholics by making clear—beyond any doubt that later naysayers might want to introduce—that we are all equal in baptism, that baptism is our entry into mission, and that as baptized members of the community we have a right and responsibility to defend the good of the church, truly to "own" the church, and to speak out forcefully if necessary when we feel that the church is in error or in danger. This does not guarantee that we are always correct in our assessment, of course. But it does mean that our words and actions, informed, prudent, and in conscience, form part of the work of the Spirit for the good of the church. How fortunate that the council made these responsibilities so clear that no bishop has yet tried to argue that the laity should return to their previously passive and acquiescent role. Or have they?

It has seemed for some time now that there are sectors of the American hierarchy that would look with equanimity, if not complacency, upon the emergence of a smaller, more "faithful," Catholic Church. This could only happen, of course, through attrition, and there is no question that there is a slow but perceptible decline in Catholic practice. Some of this is attributable to the fallout from the sex-abuse scandal and the disillusionment with the quality of episcopal leadership that came with it. Some of it undoubtedly has to do with more longstanding dissatisfactions with particular ethical teachings or with the treatment of women or gays and lesbians. Some, I am afraid, is just exhaustion, as long-term faithful Catholics give up on the fight for their church and take refuge in the Episcopal Church or the United Church of Christ or the Sunday papers. It is not an unreasonable response to a church in which altering liturgical language or reasserting the essentially different roles that laypeople and the ordained have in the celebration of the mass is apparently more important than addressing the problem of declining access to the Eucharist or the dysfunctions of clericalism.

It is now over forty years since Vatican II ended, but it remains an open question just how much its vision motivates Catholics. The more liberal and activist portions of the church are rightly described as "Vatican II Catholics," particularly the older generation who form the bulk of the membership of Catholic movements such as Call to Action and Voice of the Faithful. Most of them are now over sixty years old, many of them Vietnam veterans and people who grew up in the bewildering 1960s. Their dissatisfaction with church leadership originates in a sense, not always well defined, that somehow the vision of Vatican II has been lost, perhaps even betrayed. Younger generations, for whom Vatican II may seem less central, are often described as "voluntarist Catholics," that is, they choose Catholicism like American Protestants have always chosen their worship communities, with an enthusiasm that does not hide the fact that this is a personal choice that could change. Young Catholics, in particular, may be attached to the person of the pope or to the rediscovery of devotions that were lost for a time after the council, but their attachment to the church is in their will rather than than their blood. They are famously eclectic in their choices (note, *their* choices) of which teachings to accept and which to ignore. And while their lack of interest in their elders' constant reference to Vatican II may just be adolescent rebellion, "killing the fathers," the council's teaching remains the best way to present a vision of the church that they can embrace without inconsistency.

The task of the American Catholic Church today is to remain faithful to the spirit and the letter of Vatican II. This is the burden that lay Catholics must take on because so many of our leaders have not kept faith with the message of the council. The Second Vatican Council is the contemporary expression of Catholic orthodoxy. Its teachings are neither liberal nor conservative, but its spirit is one of openness to the world, optimism and dialogue, collaboration and coresponsibility. A church that is faithful to the vision of Vatican II will not be one in which doctrinal liberals are comfortable and doctrinal conservatives are disaffected. But it will be one in which dialogue between these different points of view is the order of the day, one that shows the world the face of an open rather than a closed society. It will be uncomfortable for people who cannot see that they must behave as adults in an adult church.

Before we turn to all these matters, there is the question of just what it means to call for adulthood, either of the church itself or of its members. Obviously enough, being adult is not just a matter of having lived so many years or passed some milestone. In that sense, most Catholics are adults. Instead, it has to do with deciding what kind of conduct deserves the label "adult," and then determining who acts in this way and who fails to act in this way. However old the person might be, childish or immature behavior disqualifies them from adulthood. The same seems to be true for institutions. To be adult, they must treat their members as adults.

One of the endemic problems of the Catholic Church is its tendency toward the infantilization of its members. Thus, we have that curious phenomenon in our church of the divided life of the layperson. She or he is an adult, with adult responsibilities and concerns. This person may be highly educated and employed in a profession requiring enormous skills and highly refined capacities for judgment. She or he probably has family responsibilities, children, and perhaps an aging parent to care for. The layperson may have a complex and demanding life. But in the church, he or she is an infant. What other word can there be for someone who is cared for by the clergy, whose needs for sustenance are met in the sacraments administered by the clergy, who is told what to think and how to behave by the clergy, and who is allowed absolutely no voice in the church, no say whatsoever in the formation of Catholic positions on religious or ethical matters? Swathed in the comforting blankets of ecclesial life, he or she is prized most when heard least, sleeping peacefully in the arms of holy mother church.

The structures of ordination/consecration and the resultant creation of a clerical oligarchy mean that the church is constantly shooting itself in the foot. Most Catholic financiers are not clergy, but all executive financial decisions in the church must in the final analysis be approved by the pastor or bishop, however little skill or taste they have for money matters. Most Catholic psychologists, therapists, and ethicists, and almost all Catholic parents are laypeople, but all formally authoritative ethical teaching is determined by a very few bishops and propagated by the rest of them. Practically all Catholics with expert knowledge of sexual dysfunctions and their attendant pathologies are laypeople. But only bishops have made judgments on how to deal with clergy guilty of sex abuse. These days the majority of trained Catholic theologians in the United States are laypeople, but doctrine is formulated by bishops with no formal input from anyone else and, even more unfortunately, with very little attention paid by the magisterium to the collective wisdom of the theological community. And, above all, most active Catholics are women, but women are excluded from the ranks of the oligarchy for one reason and one reason alone. Because they are women.

It is important to understand that the infantilization of ordinary Catholics is a feature of church structure even when it is not always something felt by this or that individual. We can see that more clearly if we imagine an ordinary lay Catholic who seems to us anything but ordinary. What is it like to be the CEO of a major corporation, possessed of significant wealth, and a good practicing Catholic who wishes to contribute something to the church that she or he loves? In some ways, it will not be the same as it is for the less affluent or the less well positioned among us. Our CEO is rather more likely than the rest of us to get a call from the bishop from time to time, perhaps asked to sit on this board or that board in the diocese, certainly approached occasionally for financial contributions. Another example might be a Catholic physician of some eminence, or a psychologist or even, God help us, a lay theologian. All these individuals might attract the attention of a bishop, perhaps for very good reasons. It might be that the bishop is a fine and well-intentioned fellow who sees the need to draw on the expertise of those outside the ranks of the clergy. But in absolutely no case will this man or woman to whom the bishop turns ever have any *formal* voice in governance or teaching. Not even if she or he is smarter or more learned or more experienced, wiser or holier. Not ever. And the reason is because he or she is not part of the clerical and clericalist establishment. Part of a priestly people perhaps, but not "a priest."

In such a structure, how can an ordinary Catholic exercise his or her responsibility to live an adult life? Vatican II seems to have called for such adulthood in its restoration of the lay state to a position of theological importance. A baptized Christian is called to an adult vocation in service of the mission of the church. Moreover, if this vocation is one lived out in the world as an individual, spreading the good news of the love of God for the world by word and force of example, it is a calling that requires no ecclesiastical approval or oversight. I live as a Christian in the world in virtue of baptism, not because some church leader has decided that it is here or there that I should serve, in this or that capacity. There is, then, an expectation of adult behavior on the part of the lay Catholic, but how can one live in an adult manner in a church in which one is formally held in an infantile relationship to its leaders?

The truth of the matter is that because of the oligarchic structure of the Catholic Church claiming adulthood must always seem strident, if not actually subversive. It is almost as if claiming adulthood in the church is a prophetic stance in itself. A Catholic who wants to have a say in the way the church organizes itself, treats its people, and presents itself to the world is not going to be welcomed with open arms by the hierarchy. If he or she is not coopted by being given a medal or being put on the bishop's advisory board, or achieving office in some Catholic charitable organization, this person is going to be labeled, sooner or later, as a troublemaker. Moreover, this status is not acquired by maintaining a heterodox position on a major doctrine of the church, or holding out for some pluralism in ethical matters. It happens simply by virtue of being unwilling to accept an ecclesiastical status quo in which all leadership, authority, and governance is held by a small, self-perpetuating minority of men.

To want an adult church, stridently or not, is to want the good of the church. While those of us who want to see a more open and accountable church with a greater role for ordinary Catholics are usually seen, at best, as rocking the boat, more commonly as those terrible "dissidents," we have sound theological and historical scholarship on our side. The church that we have today is not a perfect church. It is simply one historical moment in an ever-changing ecclesial body that does some things better than it used to, and some things worse. Scholars generally agree that responsibility for the church was much more widely shared in the first five hundred years of its existence, and most, if not all, would say that in becoming a church more and more polarized along lay/clerical lines we have lost more than we have gained. This scholarly consensus would clearly value movements for church reform much more highly than is the common view among our bishops. "Dissidents" emerge less as those who want to destroy something cherished, more as those who want to recover ancient ecclesial wisdom that time has caused us to forget, or as people with a wholly understandable concern that their church be recognized as an adult and accountable community of faith.

Before we turn to questions of change in the church, we need to take a look at the attitudes that we all should bring to the debate. Posturing, polemics, and ideological commitments are really not in place when we all seek the good of the church that we love. In the next chapter, then, we will examine some of the preconditions for a healthy public arena in which Catholics of differing convictions can make their cases.

Bibliographical Note

The literature about the Second Vatican Council is enormous, and the danger is that we will simply select from it that which satisfies our own assumptions about the importance of the council. An interesting early book that is no longer in print but can be found in libraries is the young Joseph Ratzinger's *Theological Highlights of Vat-*

ican II (Mahwah, N.J.: Paulist Press, 1966). It is very instructive to read this alongside the 1968 book by Cardinal Léon Joseph Suenens, *Coresponsibility in the Church* (New York: Herder & Herder, 1968), also no longer in print. The best recent treatment for those with limited time is *A Short History of Vatican II*, by Giuseppe Alberigo (Maryknoll, N.Y.: Orbis Books, 2006), who together with the American scholar Joseph Komonchak is the overall editor of the magisterial five-volume *History of Vatican II*, also published by Orbis Books. But in many ways the place to start is with a debate between two distinguished American Jesuits in *America* magazine (February 24, 2003). There, John O'Malley wrote "The Style of Vatican II," and Cardinal Avery Dulles countered with "Vatican II: The Myth and the Reality." For those who like Web resources, a very helpful site is that offered by a Canadian professor, Hilmar M. Pabel, to be found at http://www.sfu.ca/~pabel/ VATICAN2.HTM .

Discussion Questions

1. What does the phrase "an open church in an open society" mean to you? Is democracy in the church a value to you? How would you respond to the commonly heard phrase, "the church is not a democracy"? What do you think the limits of openness should be, if any?
2. Are there differences between the way in which adult Catholics should see their secular responsibilities to political life and the way in which they should understand their roles in the church? What are they?
3. Do you feel that the church treats you as an adult or as a child? Are there differences between the local church and the universal church in this regard?
4. How have you learned about Vatican II? How has it been presented to you? How important is it to you to learn more about the teaching of the council? What can be done to make it more accessible?

Chapter One

PRAYER, DISCERNMENT, AND DISAGREEMENT

Because most of this book will be devoted to a thorough appraisal of where we are in the church and where we are going, it is important to establish the context in which the criticisms that follow must be placed. It is all too easy to dismiss those who have things to say about the church that will be unsettling for many, and particularly so if they do not make clear that their motivations are pure. No one can be assured that they are right, of course—not those who want change nor those who want things kept exactly as they are. But there is undoubtedly a tendency in church circles to think that the latter group, let's call them the "default Catholics," need no defense of their position. After all, aren't they just being faithful to the church or its teaching? Default Catholics think that the church was created with a panoply of factory-installed "settings," conveniently divinely ordained or "laid down by Christ." In this case, variation or the desire for change seems like a virus that endangers the stability of the whole. Critics of this or that element of the church are more like customizers than default Christians. They see the factory-installed settings as a starting point from which modifications can and should constantly be made in order that things function with maximum effectiveness in changing situations. They are happy when they are exploring the potential of the software or tinkering with the hardware itself. Their opposite numbers simply want the computer to work and suspect that the tinkerers might not always know exactly what they are doing. And sometimes they are right.

Someone who does not welcome change in the church can find it easy and comforting to link a particular vision of the past, usually the recent past, with the will of God. Someone who wants change must find a way to show that what God wills for us now may not be exactly the same as what God willed for us in the recent or distant past. Even if she or he can find pastoral, historical, or theological reasons for this or that new approach, the innovator is all but defenseless in the face of attacks on personal integrity, since innovation or critique require, of their nature, that the everyday institutional framework of the church be challenged. But default Catholics take that very institutional framework to be beyond question. To take the computer analogy a little further, if there is to be change in the church, they think, if the factory-installed settings are to be changed, then the changes must be mandated by the manufacturer itself. Anything else, any appeal to the Spirit or the freedom of the children of God, is simply a cover for irresponsible tinkering and will result in things running less effectively or—in the worst case—cause the church, like the computer, to crash.

That the church just might crash if we do not do something to upgrade some elements of it is one way of stating the argument of this book. It is, inevitably, a position that draws a lot of ire and not a little contempt from those who think of the church as unchanging. In the chapters that follow we will have occasion to explain what we propose and to defend its wisdom, knowing always that we are not infallible. But in this opening chapter we need to arm ourselves against the charge that we are destructive or faithless or motivated by whatever deplorable set of feelings. Otherwise, the capacity to look fairly at our critique and the proposals that go with it is simply preempted. Why would you listen to someone who is busy trying to destroy the church that you love? But just suppose that they are moved by the same love of the church as you are. Then maybe, just maybe, they should be given a hearing.

In the remainder of this chapter we need to look at the common ground upon which stand all Catholics who are concerned about the future of their church. Only by so doing can we avoid the arid polarizations that seem to plague the church these days. The church in Europe and increasingly in North America is going through a very difficult time for all kinds of reasons, some of them unconnected to religion. Labels like conservative and liberal, though they will be used here, are often unhelpful, if only because they tend to be linked in our minds with the political meanings of the terms. But just as behind the differences that mark our secular politics we are all Americans who care deeply about the future of our country, though we may have different visions of what that should be, so liberal and conservative Catholics are similarly driven by a concern for the vitality of their communities of faith. We may in the end not be able to reconcile all the disagreements, but we can certainly avoid unnecessary divisiveness. Marking the important things that should bind us together is one way to do so. In the remainder of this chapter we need to look closely at three truths that are equally important for all concerned Catholics. We all need to pray. We desperately need the skills of discernment, through which we can refine our sense of how our convictions incorporate both feelings and rational analysis. And then we need to recognize that we will disagree with one another, at least some of the time, and that there are ways to do that which reflect a love of the church rather than a fascination with our own opinions.

Prayer

There is no genuine prayer in which we do not stand before God in humility, knowing that we need divine grace. Jesus gives us the best possible example of genuine prayer when he contrasts the Pharisee and the publican (Luke 18:9-14). The Pharisee, you will remember, enters the synagogue to thank God that he is "not as other men." Let us suppose that he is right in evaluating himself as better than average. He has good reason to do so, because he sees the signs; he tithes, gives alms, and so on. These are fine things to do. And as a Pharisee, he is a member of a lay reform movement within rabbinic Judaism; he is not an obscurantist. Let us suppose too that he is genuinely grateful to God for the blessings of being above average. Nothing in the text suggests that he is insincere, though he certainly seems to be a little judgmental. Turning to the publican, we meet someone whose employment made him both hated and feared in Israel. Biblical "publicans" were people employed by the Romans to collect taxes, and who used others in something rather like a protection racket to extort more than the Romans had levied. So it would be a fair assumption that his life outwardly is not as ethical as that of the Pharisee. We do not know if he gives alms or keeps everything he has for himself. We are certainly not led by the gospel story to think that he is the better man. We are simply supposed to recognize that his is the better prayer. Why? For two reasons. The first and more obvious reason is that he recognizes his sinfulness, that he knows he is in need of divine assistance and mercy. But a second reason adds some color and context to the first. The publican stands before God alone. That is why he is so aware that he is a sinner. Facing God, our sinfulness can be apparent only to us. But the Pharisee situates his prayer relative to the qualities of those others from whom he thanks God for distancing him. He is a little bit like those of our fellow citizens who defend America against criticism by saying that the other side behaves worse. The Pharisee compares himself to other people, and perhaps he is right that he is above average. But that is irrelevant to prayer. Prayer is being in the presence of God as a sinner who knows that he or she needs God's grace. In prayer we are alone with God. Only this explains the constant refrain of the holiest saints that they are the lowliest sinners. They are not comparing themselves to those around them; then their protestations would be simply ridiculous. They are standing before God, where their need for grace is all that counts. Surely, prayer can also be prayer for things and certainly for others. But prayer does not legitimately include editorializing and is not best conducted through a catalog of my accomplishments relative to those of others.

Both liberals and conservatives pray. Both groups, default Catholics and the customizers, are open to making the same mistakes as the Pharisee. That is, our prayer can become a matter of asking God that those other people be converted, or see the light, or leave the church, or whatever it is that we imagine will make our church better and our lot in life a happier one. All this is Pharisee prayer because it is about other people, not about ourselves. We all need to pray like the publican. The ideology or point of view that we hold on issues of church discipline or married clergy ought not to intrude in our prayer. Liberals and conservatives ought to be praying the same prayer: "God be merciful to me, a sinner." In this perfect prayer is the recognition that God loves us, that we shall never merit the love of God, and that God's grace can transform us, even when and perhaps especially because we cannot merit it. Keeping such prayer firmly in our minds is a marvelous way to filter out both pride and false humility, either of which will cloud our judgments.

If what moves us to pray like the publican is humility, the fruit of the publican's prayer is confidence. When we pray the prayer of trust in God's mercy and transforming power, we become strong because we recognize that our strength comes from God and not from our own power. Our source of confidence, the strength that comes from depending on God, constantly reminds us of the need for humility. The publican's prayer works a bit like Lake Wobegon's Powdermilk Biscuits, which "give shy people the strength to get up and do what needs to be done, even if it's just to sit down and shut up." In fact, the theology of Garrison Keillor's astoundingly well-imagined world of rural Minnesota can shed a bit more light. The old-time gospel and "family values" that flavor "The Prairie Home Companion" underpin both the social conservatism of the majority and the outspoken political radicalism of Keillor himself. What binds him to his world of Lake Wobegon is not that he shares a political position with the denizens of the Chatterbox Café, but that they are all aware that they are in need of divine assistance. He disagrees with most of them, but he evidently loves them all.

Discernment

Because neither liberals nor conservatives have the lock on sincerity, and both can speak at times out of fear or anger or plain old meanness, the gift of discernment is vital to those who feel impelled to speak out for the good of the church. Because we are not infallible, we have to be able to recognize where we are being moved by the spirit of God and where baser motives or selfish inclinations may be at work, where we are filled with love, and where fear or anger may have intruded. Of course, we are not always the best judges in our own cases. It is all too easy to determine that the Holy Spirit's inclinations dovetail conveniently with our own. This is one reason why Ignatius of Loyola, one of the great spiritual teachers of the art of discernment, recommended the services of a spiritual director to help individuals in the process of "discernment of spirits," the term he used for the complex psychological dynamics of authentic self-determination.

St. Ignatius's fundamental rule for discernment can be boiled down to something like "listen to your heart but use your head." Perhaps there is a former Jesuit working for the marketing division of BMW. One of their current advertising lines certainly sounds like it—"Drive with your heart but buy with your head!"—and most people could use some discernment when they are purchasing a new automobile. Of course, Ignatius is talking about discerning how the spirits are moving us internally, toward the good or away from it. He sees that well-intentioned people do not always make good decisions. Anyone who goes through Ignatius's *Spiritual Exercises* can be assumed to be well intentioned, but a generous spirit still needs to learn to listen to the interior voices that will give specificity to the call to a deeper commitment to Christ. Anyone who ever set out on the long road to priesthood or solemn profession in a religious order knows that sometimes discernment leads the individual to see that what God wills is something different from what she or he imagines is the case. And there is no better example of the need for discernment than the prospect of marriage, an affair of the heart that could often use more cool reason than is usually employed.

Ignatius's "Rules for the Discernment of Spirits" are offered in the context of the *Spiritual Exercises*, and so might reasonably and rightly be assumed to take for granted a foundational security in the faith of the church. Committed Christians, however, are not immune to psychological processes or the struggle between self-centeredness and other-centeredness that marks the universal human condition. Knowing this, Ignatius is insistent that in all decision making we need to keep firmly in mind the purpose of our creation: to praise God and to save one's soul. It is wrong, he says, to choose a state of life such as the priesthood or marriage and then determine to serve God in that state. The correct order is to place one's salvation firmly in the front of one's mind, and then to ask what state in life best favors this more fundamental purpose.

While Ignatius would not have applied his rules directly to the situation of someone trying to understand how to reform the church, his rules work well in this context. Liberal or conservative, our concern has to be for the good of the church that it enable the praise of God, and for our own integrity relative to the church. While all of us are perhaps temperamentally more conservative or more liberal, and it is good for us to know where we stand here, it would be wrong in Ignatius's view for us to come to the question of the good of the church and our own souls with a prior *ideological* commitment to the left or the right. What matters when we engage in debate over particular church concerns is not a slavish favoritism for liberal or conservative solutions but a firm and unswerving conviction that we will pursue the good of the church. Of course, as Ignatius would be quick to tell us, the evil spirit can mislead us into advocating evil rather than good, and we need to learn to know how the spirits move us to what he calls "consolation"—or "every increase in faith, hope, and love"—and "desolation"—or whatever leads to "want of faith, want of hope, want of love."

The art of discernment will teach us to suspect our own motives, to listen to our hearts, and to evaluate the evidence that is available to support or to contradict our inclinations on any particular issue. But most of all, it provides us with a ground upon which we are willing to take on the responsibilities of challenging the church to praise God better. Just so long as we are motivated rightly and savvy about the ways in which we can be misled into simply favoring our own inclinations, we can then proceed to be faithful critics of this or that, with a pure heart and a cheerful spirit. Consolation is signaled by feelings of peace and drawing closer to God, desolation by anxiety and melancholy, and the move away from God. How do these warring impulses play out in the common experience among Catholics today of deep disagreements about the church?

Disagreement

If we have learned to pray more like the publican than the Pharisee, and if we have acquired at least some facility in discerning the ways in which good and evil impulses sometimes conflict within us, we should not assume that disagreements will never occur within the community of faith. There are a number of reasons why prayer and discernment do not lead to unanimity. One is that different personalities will naturally lean in different directions on contested issues. Some people may simply be more adventurous than others, though being adventurous may be exactly the right thing to do in one situation and quite the wrong thing in another. But the more fundamental explanation for disagreement among Catholics is that there are many matters on which a variety of points of view are legitimate. Some of these things will be sufficiently unimportant that we can simply agree to differ, and legitimate and even healthy pluralism will result. For example, there are different opinions about the timing of confirmation, the best way to teach the fundamentals of Catholicism to children, the importance of prayers like the rosary, or devotions like benediction or exposition of the Blessed Sacrament, and so on. But disagreements can also occur in areas where unanimity would be a good thing but where the tradition is going through processes of more or less rapid change. That is, doctrine is developing, perhaps even dramatically; and people filled with good intentions, while necessarily leaning one way or the other, are caught up in the process of change, too close to it for total confidence that this or that perspective is correct. Examples of this kind of challenge have varied over the course of history. The practice of lending money at interest was considered immoral. The wisdom of the Crusades or the morality of slavery are other good examples from previous moments in history. In our times most of the examples we have to deal with are ethical or ecclesiological. The debate over birth control in the 1960s and '70s was a recent good example, while today perhaps we could cite the question of the admission of the divorced and remarried to the Eucharist, or the complex issues surrounding what is sometimes called "the right to die," or the ongoing debate over the wisdom of maintaining mandatory celibacy for diocesan clergy.

The point of all this is that disagreement is natural, even inevitable in a church committed as ours is to the notion that doctrine develops, that we live in a changing church in a changing world. But it is also true that these disagreements can be painful to some and can also sometimes be unnecessarily negative, either because they lead to personal attacks by one side against the other, or perhaps because they are products of ignorance. When we study the issue of papal infallibility, for example, we rapidly discover that it is not the magical power that some of its most vociferous proponents would like it to be, nor is it the embarrassment that liberals often imagine. And when Catholics in recent decades locked horns over *Humanae Vitae*, it was not a battle between those who were against sex and those who were obsessed with sex, but rather an honest disagreement about how marital love is best lived out.

Disagreement in the church is a sign of health, provided that it is accompanied by prayer and discernment, but there is a need for some ground rules for the adult practice of disagreement. Ground rules are required because disagreement in the church is not just between two groups of people who feel strongly on an issue. The church also teaches, though of course its teaching is sometimes in the process of development too. But more often than not, one side in the disagreement can invoke the teaching authority of the church in its behalf. This argument from authority is not irrelevant and on fundamental matters of Catholic doctrine is comfortably acceptable to people of all points of view. In the common areas of disagreement in the church, however, we are not dealing with fundamental doctrines; and consequently the recourse to the argument from authority can seem to be a ploy to foreclose discussion and win the argument. It is also a matter of simple fact that the argument from authority is employed much more often from the more conservative standpoint, for the simple reason that their position is most often the one that current teaching supports. Liberals, of course, will counter that in a tradition that believes in doctrinal development the official position of the church will naturally always lag behind the dialogical process through which understanding grows. If this were not at least sometimes the case, then doctrine would never develop at all. As Cardinal John Henry Newman wrote in his great nineteenth-century essay on the development of doctrine, "to live is to change."

Three ground rules for the healthy exercise of ecclesial disagreement recommend themselves. The first is that there should be a level playing field on which the tussles between differing points of view are played out. The second is that church teaching is always subject to the process of reception; in other words, what is said must be said in a way in which it can be heard and accepted. And the third is that in the last analysis, the Holy Spirit cannot be at war with itself; or, in a debate between faithful Catholics in whom the Spirit of God is at work, any outcome that leaves the two sides totally unreconciled with each other cannot be the work of the Spirit. These three rules speak respectively to the conditions that should exist if a healthy debate is to occur, to the use of authority in the conduct of the debate, and to the ways in which the outcomes of the debate can be evaluated.

Ground rule one states that in areas where disagreement exists and a debate is under way, if the truth is to emerge, it is most important that those who disagree do so on a level playing field. The exercise of ecclesiastical power or the premature recourse to an argument from authority in order to foreclose discussion is unhelpful. Of course, the teaching authority of the church has the right and responsibility to delimit those areas in which legitimate disagreement can occur, but when it does this it needs to submit itself to the standards that any good teacher would employ. The magisterium is not *in loco parentis* and should not employ the harassed father's nuclear option, "Because I said so!" As daddy soon discovers, in any case, this doesn't work very well as the children mature and looks simply foolish when the children are grown up. In an adult and accountable church the argument from authority should be employed very sparingly. A good teacher knows what it is that she wants her students to learn, but also knows the difference between rote learning and the real learning that occurs when the student makes it her own. Good teachers trust the truth and do not confuse it with their own positions, still less with their own authority.

Ground rule number two maintains that to step back from the abuse of authority is not at all to abandon the effort to teach the tradition, but rather to recognize that if students are to learn effectively, what is taught must be true and it must be taught effectively. The church—particularly the bishop—teaches. However—to stay with the analogy of the good classroom teacher a little longer—an effective teacher takes into account the context of the students. In the jargon of pedagogy these days this is sometimes called student-centered learning, but good teachers have always done it. Just getting up in

front of people and reading a lecture is a pretty sure way to be inef-
fective. A good teacher knows that if the students are well intentioned
and willing to do the work but they do not "get it," then "it" is not
being communicated effectively. Bad teachers are usually too ready
to blame the students.

In Catholic theology the issue we are dealing with is discussed as
"reception" or even "reception theory." It begins from the recognition
that something must be taught in a manner in which the learners can
"hear" the teaching. All the lessons about good teachers discussed
above come into play here. But reception theory goes further to ask
what is going on when the teaching is not heard. If faithful and well-
intentioned adult Catholics who practice the prayer of the publican
and have some ability to discern the way the spirits are moving them
fail in large numbers to receive a teaching, what does this say about
the teaching? We cannot immediately jump to the conclusion that it
is erroneous teaching, though that remains a possibility. We must first
examine the possibility that the problem lies with the way in which it
is being taught. Let's take a look at an example. In the American
Catholic Church today, and frankly in most parts of the world, the
majority of laypeople who go to church on a regular basis favor an end
to mandatory celibacy for parochial clergy. Surveys of Catholic public opinion regularly show that between 65 and 75 percent of those
questioned support an end to the current law. Mandatory celibacy in
the Roman church is not an article of faith, though it is a practice
sanctioned by almost a thousand years of use. The official position of
the church on the matter is that although mandatory celibacy is not
an article of faith, it is and will remain the law of the church that diocesan clergy make a promise of celibacy. How do we evaluate this situation? On the one hand, it is certainly not sufficient to say that on a
matter that is not an article of faith a simple majority opinion is correct. They could be mistaken. Nor, on the other hand, can one say that
the chronological duration of the practice is determinative. The
church was comfortable with slavery for close to two thousand years,
but that did not make it right. It seems clear that we can say with confidence that if "good Catholics" do not "get it," then the onus is on the
teaching church to explore better ways to propose and support their
position. And, perhaps, if efforts to clarify the teaching or communi-

cate it more effectively subsequently fail, the time will come when the question has to be asked, "Are we teaching the wrong thing?"

This question brings us to the third ground rule for healthy disagreement, namely, that "the Spirit cannot be at war with itself." Human beings can quite successfully frustrate the workings of the Holy Spirit, of course. The action of the Holy Spirit can never just be assumed to be identical with "whatever happens." Then the Spirit would seem to side with evil from time to time, or be complicit in poor decision making. But it does seem likely that the Holy Spirit would be active in a process of debate conducted on all sides by people of prayer and discernment, oriented to determining what is for the good of the church, and conducted on a level playing field in which arguments from authority or other power plays are not utilized. To quote Ignatius of Loyola once again, debate should intend "that the truth should appear, and not that we should seek to gain the upper hand." In the best of all possible worlds this kind of debate would then be what the German sociologist Jürgen Habermas calls an "ideal-speech situation," and then the Holy Spirit would be happy with any outcome. But in our sin-tainted world something always prevents the ideal speech situation from occurring, and the Spirit may be hampered or wounded.

The more sensitive point that has to be made is that there is no exact equivalency between the teaching of the church and the voice of the Spirit. At times in the past the leaders of the church have been wrong, and the rank and file have been where the Spirit has taken up residence. If that has happened in the past, it could happen today. It could be happening now. Vatican II allowed for this possibility when it wrote of the faith of the whole church as possessing a kind of infallibility. That is, the faithful express the infallibility of the church through their practice, as the bishops together or sometimes even the pope alone can exercise that same infallibility through their direct teaching. Infallibility in the end is nothing other than the fulfillment of God's promise of the guidance of the Spirit, and Vatican II saw it differently played out in the roles of the pope, the whole college of the bishops, and the whole faithful. The fact that the Spirit cannot be at war with itself and that we have historical examples of times when the leaders of the church were wrong and the people were the guardians of the gospel (the most famous being in the Arian controversies of the fourth century) means that we cannot simply say that the magisterium is always able to claim infallibly to discern whether the Spirit is or is not speaking through the practice of the whole faithful people.

Faithful conservatives and faithful liberals love the church. But you cannot identify the church with any one segment, not with liberals or conservatives certainly, but also not with the pope or the hierarchy or the people. You have to love the whole sorry mess, all those who are with you in praying the prayer of the publican, and even those who are not. Identification of the church with the pope is an error. Identification of the church with the bishops or with the laity is an error. Love of the church, in other words, is not like loving chocolate or loving champagne. It is not the love of an object that we possess or desire to possess. Love of the church is one sinner's act of solidarity with a sinful people, united in their common dependence on the grace of God for their salvation. Loving the church, we all want it to be more and better in its faithfulness to the gospel. But just because love of the church is not love of an object that we might possess but an act of solidarity, the desire that the church grow in faithfulness has to be carried out in community, in dialogue where there is disagreement. We must know the difference between where we can agree to differ and where we must keep talking—always, of course, seeking the truth of the gospel and not our own advantage; always speaking honestly and even forthrightly but always aware that our own judgments are revisable; always willing the good of the other; always loving those with whom we are in profound disagreement; always purifying our intentions through the prayer of the publican; and always trusting our hearts but using our heads.

Bibliographical Note

St. Ignatius's rules for the discernment of spirits can be found in any edition of his *Spiritual Exercises*, nos. 314–36. Those who would like to follow up on the Ignatian notion of discernment might look at the relevant essays in *The Way of Ignatius Loyola: Contemporary*

Approaches to the Spiritual Exercises, edited by Philip Sheldrake (St. Louis: Institute of Jesuit Sources, 1991). For a gentle introduction to how to disagree in the church and remain calm and sane, there is no better resource than Donald Cozzens's book, *Faith That Dares to Speak* (Collegeville, Minn.: Liturgical Press, 2004). For an important statement of more centrist or even moderately conservative younger Christian theologians on dialogue and church teaching, try the somewhat more challenging essays in *New Wine, New Wineskins: A Next Generation Reflects on Key Issues in Catholic Moral Theology*, edited by William C. Mattison III (Lanham, Md.: Rowman & Littlefield, 2005). Finally, the idea of "dramatically developing" tradition comes from John Thiel's book *Senses of Tradition* (New York: Oxford, 2000).

Discussion Questions

1. Is the distinction helpful between "default Catholics" and Catholic computer geeks who like to tinker with the factory-installed settings? Where would you place yourself? Is there some middle position, and how could it be articulated?
2. To what extent do you think that praying together might be a source of renewal in a divided church? Does this happen in your own faith community? Is it possible?
3. If we are all, conservatives and liberals, honestly pursuing the good of the church, what does it mean for us to have major disagreements? How can we get past them?
4. In your own experience, what aspects of the church's teaching or the manner of teaching make it difficult for you to "receive" or "hear" the teaching? What could be done to fix this?

Chapter Two

THE ROLE OF THE LAITY

In a course on the theology of the laity it is always instructive to get students to see the central issue at stake by throwing down a challenge on day one. "What we have to discover is a definition of a layperson that does *not* use the word 'not'!" You might not be surprised to hear that this is quite a difficult task, though obviously not impossible, or we would have to give up on the course and any theology of the laity. The obvious ways of identifying laypeople use the n-word all the time. "Laypeople are *not* priests." "They are *not* in positions of leadership in the church"; or "they can*not* say mass"; or "they can*not* preach"; or "they are *not* obliged to celibacy." The trouble with all such efforts is that they are not definitions, which must always have a positive content. They are descriptions. As descriptions of the life of laypeople in the church today they are accurate as far as they go, but since they work by excluding something or other they don't provide any material on which to reflect. And if you can't reflect on something, you can't do theology. Theology is neither more nor less than reflecting on something in the light of the gospel and the traditions of the church, with an eye to the life of the Christian in the world of today.

The descriptions that people naturally offer when they are asked about what a layperson is are an accurate reflection of the place that laypeople find themselves in after 2,000 years of church history. Perhaps what people don't always realize is that they are in no way descriptive of something that has always been the case, or that must necessarily always remain this way. Once upon a time everyone in the church was described as a member of the laity. That happened once, and it could happen again. There was a time when lay theologians were taken very seriously by the teaching authority of the church. If we are to believe the apostle Paul, there was a time when women hosted local assemblies of Christians and perhaps presided at the meal in memory of Jesus. There was certainly a time when ministers were married, when laypeople helped choose bishops and took an active part in ecumenical councils. These things were part of the church once, and they could be again. You certainly can't say that any or all of these phenomena are essential to the church. We don't *have* to have married priests or deaconesses. But you can say that since we have had them in the past, they cannot contradict anything essential to the church. So, they could become part of the church's life once again.

What Are "Laity"?

The very early church never talked about "laity" and "clergy." Everyone was a part of the *laos* or "people" of God. So, long before there were clergy and laity, there were simply Christians. In the days of Jesus himself, he had followers, some of whom he called and some of whom simply attached themselves to him, before he ever named apostles. In the early years after Pentecost the first followers of Jesus thought of themselves as a sect of Judaism and were thought by the Jews to be such a group, at least if we are to believe the Acts of the Apostles. So, before there was a church, there were followers of Jesus the Nazarene. The formation of "the church" as we know it is a somewhat protracted process, which begins as the followers of Jesus, moved by the Spirit, imagine life without him. The early letters of Paul, the oldest documents in the New Testament, show some of the experimental character and even the chaos that marked these first few decades. In the letters of Paul and the Gospels that followed, there is no hint of "clergy" and "laity" as we know them today. To be clearer: there are certainly some leadership roles that are played out by particular individuals and not by others as, for instance, in the plentiful evidence from the greetings in Pauline letters that women were major figures in at least some of the "household churches," which seem to have been the earliest venues for the celebration of the Lord's Supper. Scholars disagree about just how early a clear distinction comes to be made between clergy and laity, though no one, as far as I know, is willing to date it before the second century. And they all agree that in the very early church, even when the distinction was made, it implied no classification of people into ranks, even more clearly no assignment of particular holiness to one group or another. In the early church, the mark of holiness was baptism, not ordination. The *whole* church, the *whole* people of God, was set apart for the service of the Lord.

Let's return for a moment to the problem of defining laypeople positively. A more sophisticated attempt to do so might avoid the negatives and say something like, "they are baptized Christians called to ministry." True enough, even if forgotten for many centuries, and wholly in the spirit both of the early church and of Vatican II. While this accurately depicts the place of laypeople in the church, it does not distinguish them, however, from the clergy. Indeed, this is so precisely because such a definition harks back to those early days when the distinction made no sense. It leaves us with essentially the same problem of explaining how they are called to ministry in ways differing from the ways that the clergy are called, without the call seeming to be a lesser call. But in the historical development of the church, this is exactly what happened. As the roles of priests and bishops became more and more distinct, the roles of laypeople were diminished, if not always demeaned.

While the history of the changing fortunes of the laity is complex and drawn out over several centuries, the fundamental reason for it is fairly simple and wholly without sinister intent. Suppose that all M&Ms were the same color, except that every bag contained one purple and one white M&M. Which would gain more attention? Which would be sought out more eagerly? Which would likely be suspected to have greater flavor or more distinctiveness? About which M&M

would we ask, "Why is it here? What is its meaning?" It is always the special, not the run of the mill, that garners the attention, and this is no different in the life of the church or in Christian theology, since both are sites of human behavior. So, as some individuals showed talents for leadership or preaching or religious reflection or holiness, over a period of time it was natural that they would come to be looked up to. Over time, the church would naturally tend to define their positions and, indeed, their privileges and responsibilities. Bishops, somehow successors of the apostles who led the very early church, were obviously important. Eventually, a couple of centuries later, with the rise of the monastic movement, monks too would be seen to be special and understood somehow to represent an ideal of the Christian life, though obviously not one that all or most were suited for. And laypeople, those who were not special in gifts of leadership or learning or holiness, would just be forgotten. Certainly, they were not abandoned by the church, but they came to be seen as the recipients of what those with special gifts had to offer, rather than as persons vested with any particular responsibilities of their own or possessing any special gifts. But they were certainly forgotten by theology. They were simply not interesting enough.

Fifteen hundred years after the erasure of laypeople from the consciousness of Christian theology and from pretty much any responsible activity in church leadership, at the beginning of the twentieth century, we can see in the words of Pope St. Pius X exactly where this ended up:

> It follows that the Church is essentially an unequal society, that is, a society comprising two categories of person, the Pastors and the flock, those who occupy a rank in the different degrees of the hierarchy and the multitude of the faithful. So distinct are these categories that with the pastoral body only rests the necessary right and authority for promoting the end of the society and directing all its members towards that end; the one duty of the multitude is to allow themselves to be led and, like a docile flock, to follow the Pastors. (*Vehementer Nos,* para. 8)

There is really no better indication of the effective exclusion of the laity from the gifts of the Spirit, at least in the consciousness of the institutional church, than that chilling statement that it is the "one duty of the multitude . . . to allow themselves to be led." What has baptism become in this vision of the church, if not simply admission to the ranks of the sheep?

At the beginning of the twentieth century, under the papacy of Pius X, the thinking church was suffering enormous repression. As a result of his crusade against what was labeled "the Modernist Crisis," theological reflection that was in any way creative became intensely suspect. But as is often the way, there was a backlash against these crimes against the intellect, and theology actually emerged stronger than it had been for many centuries. For particular historical reasons, it was in France and Germany above all that the "new theology," as its enemies sarcastically referred to it, began to draw attention to the importance of good historical scholarship. One of these theologians, the French Dominican Yves Congar, gave particular attention to restoring the idea that there is a theological value to the lay state. Under his influence the fathers of the Second Vatican Council also addressed the role of the laity and came to the same conclusions Congar had reached in 1953. The particularly distinguishing mark of the layperson is his or her "secularity."

The idea that laypeople are distinctive because of their secularity was an important step forward in understanding just what a layperson was, but it was also true that without careful explanations, it could create more problems than it solved. Understood too literally, it could easily be taken to mean that here was the church and there was the world, that the normal work of the clergy was within the church, and that of laypeople in the world. The clergy dealt with the sacred, or the things of God, and the laypeople, with the secular, or the things of the world. Even understood less rigidly, along the lines that Congar and Vatican II had intended, while this language gave laypeople an important role in the mission of the church, spreading the gospel in the world by word and example, it also inevitably maintained the subordination that laypeople had been subjected to for almost fifteen hundred years. The church *itself*, one might be inclined to say, and certainly its governance, remained wholly in the hands of the clergy, as it does de facto to this day.

At about the time the Vatican Council was incorporating the ideas of Congar on the secularity of the laity, the great Dominican himself was having second thoughts, which found their way into the second edition of his wonderful book *Laypeople in the Church* and into a series of essays that he wrote for a number of French theological journals. In these works Congar criticizes first his own intellectual rigidity in making the distinction between laity and clergy too forcefully, and especially for defining the laity relative to the clergy. In other words, Congar thought he had fallen into the trap of thinking of the clergy as what we today might call "the default mode" of being Christian, with the consequence that laypeople's ways of being Christian were understood as a variation on this default status. Indeed, he said very clearly that in his view the time had been reached at which it was necessary to understand the clergy relative to the laity. Laypersons express the default mode of being Christian, and the clergy must be explained relative to them.

Congar's principal suggestion was that we should stop talking about laypeople and clergy and talk instead of "different ministries," some of which were recognized by the church in ordination, and some of which were simply empowered by the Spirit of God among all the baptized. In his own times, he was probably thinking of laypeople conducting two sorts of ministry. One, solely authorized by their baptism, is the "ministry of word and good example" that lay Catholics bring to the world in their everyday lives. The other, now no longer as significant in Catholic life as it was fifty years ago, was "Catholic Action," the name for apostolic associations of Catholics, working under ecclesiastical supervision, that had as their agenda to spread the gospel in the "secular" world. But his suggestions are considerably more valuable today in an American church in which the concept of the "ecclesial lay minister" has become so prominent. So long as we stay with the lay/clergy divide, lay ecclesial ministers must be seen as a kind of monster, or as a temporary expedient for a shortage of priests (the so-called apostolate of the second string). But once we grasp the idea of different ministries, of ordained and non-ordained ministries on a spectrum, we find lay ecclesial ministers as a permanent and valid phenomenon in their own right distinctly less difficult to envisage.

As Vatican II came to an end in 1965, this was the complex situation of the laity. Laypeople had become noticed again in the official teaching of the church. The church had recognized formally their equal dignity with clergy in virtue of their baptism and their responsibilities for the mission of the church. The council fathers had even said that laypeople had a right and responsibility to speak out when they deemed the good of the church to be imperiled, and that the clergy should listen to what they had to say. The council laid down the groundwork for the enormous growth of lay ecclesial ministers in the half century since it ended deliberations, a growth that has been more noticeable in the North American church than elsewhere. There was, however, another and less satisfactory side to the story. Apart from the passages about equal baptismal dignity and the characterization of the lay vocation as "secular," the council did not choose to reflect theologically on what it meant to be a layperson. Instead, the council fathers chose the easier path of discussing what laypeople could do in the church. In all probability, this was a result of the recognition among the bishops that a theology of the laity would get them into pretty deep waters, because it would have implications for the theological status of the ordained and even for understanding the essential character of the church as communion, which they certainly had proclaimed. And so, inevitably, the divide between clergy and laity persisted, in spite of the advances of Vatican II.

The bishops' discussion of the lay apostolate might not have been accompanied by an equally serious consideration of the theological status of lay life, but it certainly opened the door for a measure of maturation in the church, as laypeople began to play more and more significant roles. Today we have far more laypeople in positions of responsibility in chancery offices, in the Vatican, and above all in the parishes than could ever have been envisaged only fifty years ago. The Catholic laity are much more highly educated than they were a few generations ago, and for many of them that includes considerable theological education. Add to this the serious shortage of ordained clergy, and the pressure is clearly on for a radical revision of how we see the role of laypeople in the church today. In a word, laypeople have to be and to be recognized as adult. Adulthood, of course, implies ownership and requires the recognition on the part of everyone that adults make decisions for themselves. This brings the adult lay church of today into head-on confrontation with the structures of clericalism, though not with all the clergy. The clericalist church of the recent and not-so-recent past cannot coexist comfortably with an adult laity. Where adults do not make their own decisions, they are either phantom adults or they live in a paternalistic culture in which adulthood is not really recognized.

It is clear that in today's American church we are trying to find our way to adulthood in this deeper sense. Of course, the church is an organism in which different people exercise different gifts, and not all are called to leadership or to preaching, or to presidency at the Eucharist. But at the same time we all know what an adult society is like. It is one in which we have leaders with particular responsibilities, but this does not preclude a vigorous public forum in which all the adult members of the given society exercise their adult rights and responsibilities. In other words, while the church is certainly not the state, nor needs to be modeled on the state, a church which recognizes the adulthood of its members is going to need to look like any other open society. In this sense at least, the church needs to be much more democratic. The only alternative to that is the prolongation of a paternalistic culture of clericalism in which adult Catholic laypeople settle for the ecclesiastical status of children, however complex, professional, and "adult" their secular responsibilities may be.

Let us return to the question of the chapter. What is a layperson anyway? It seems that we have two possible directions in which we can go, both of which must begin with recognizing the equal dignity of all the baptized, ordained or not, and the responsibilities that all of us have for the mission of the church. The first direction, which when we are at our best we are currently employing and which we find both in early Congar and in the documents of Vatican II, sees a layperson as a baptized Christian, gifted by the Spirit with a responsibility for the mission of the church that will be carried out through the particular human qualities and gifts that this individual possesses. He or she is called to an active and responsible faith, in collaboration with the clergy and under the guidance of the teaching authority of the church vested in the bishops. Some of the laity may be called to work within the community of the faithful, though the majority will find their ministry in the world. The second direction we might go, following the hints offered by the later Congar, is to think of all the baptized as ministers in different ways, depending on their gifts. Some work within the body of the faithful, some outside it. Within the body, some are called to preside at Eucharist, some to preach, some to teach, and so on. While the ceremony of ordination is reserved for certain ministries and not for others, this direction is less comfortable in its use of the language of clergy and laity. And the principal difference between the two approaches outlined here is that the first is inclined toward maintaining an essential difference between laity and clergy, while the latter sees Christians on a spectrum, with no essential difference between what one kind of minister does and what another kind of minister does. In the first model, a layperson continues to be, in the end, defined as "not clergy." In the second, we would have to say that there are no longer clergy and laity, only the *laos,* or "people" of God.

Resistance to the second model as we have discussed it here can and often does take the form of a simple determination to maintain a cultic priesthood distinguished by lifestyle. There may be cogent arguments for maintaining that priests must be men, though I have never heard any. And there may be good reasons why priesthood should entail celibacy, though I do not know of any. But we can be pretty confident that there is no way to justify clerical culture as an essential characteristic of ordained ministry. Clerical culture does not say anything about what it means to be a priest. It is simply a description of a particular and entirely accidental subculture of Catholic life, which for historical reasons has grown up around bishops and priests. As a description it is a neutral term. But it has a dark side, usually called "clericalism," which is what has happened to clerical culture when it came to be seen as essential to the condition of priesthood. The way priesthood is lived out in the church today—

which of course is not at all the way it was always or is everywhere lived out—comes to be represented as the way it always must be. So prayers for vocations are pretty well all about celibate men.

The other and more serious objection to any efforts to blur the distinction between clergy and laity stems from a theological understanding of the sacrament of orders as conferring a "substantial ontological change" on the newly ordained priest. This was a medieval development in the church's thinking, in which ordination was thought to change the very being of the new priest. Because the change had taken place at that level, it could not be reversed, in somewhat the same way as the church has tended to understand the indissolubility of marriage. Once married, always married. Once a priest, always a priest. Hence the Catholic claim that there really is no such thing as an ex-priest. There are resigned priests or, as the church prefers, "laicized priests" (the canonical designation is actually "reduced to the lay state," which in itself should give laypeople pause for thought). But they are never really ex-priests. If they say mass, the mass is unlawful, but the consecration is valid. If they are called on in an emergency, they are expected to give absolution to a dying person. Their priestly "faculties," which come with ordination, can only be suspended, never entirely taken away. This whole set of issues surrounding the question of substantial versus relational ontological change is complex but significant, and we will return to it in more detail in chapter 4.

Ministry in the church has nothing to lose from a reframing of ordination and vocation, but clericalism is mightily threatened by it. The language of ontological change, true or not, encourages the development of a priestly caste, especially when the lifestyle of clergy in the Western church is also distinctive by its celibacy. Over the centuries, the role of the whole people, not only in selecting pastors but also and most importantly in confirming the claim to the possession of a vocation, has been entirely lost. A "vocation" to the priesthood today is an almost self-authenticating claim and determined entirely between the individual and ecclesiastical authorities. Moreover, priesthood must be one of the few professions where the claimed "vocation" precedes any real evidence that the skills required for a successful pastor are actually talents that the individual possesses. Every pastor who shuts himself away and does not interact with the people, or who lords it over them, or who preaches or presides lazily or badly is demonstrating that his claim to possess a vocation is at best questionable.

If clerical culture needs to bow to normal standards of human life for the discernment of a calling, the more fundamental problem with an emphasis on ontological change in the ordination of a priest has to do with the way in which it ties the very being of the person to what is, when all is said and done, a role in the church at the service of the people of God—not a medal or a transfer into another or higher order of being. It really is not possible to be more a Christian than any other baptized person. Baptism makes you a Christian. God may call you to certain ways of service to the church, but it does not make you *more* something. It simply gives you a particular role in the church, always in relation to the whole faithful people. Consequently, any phenomenon such as clerical culture or its wicked stepsister, *clericalism,* which possesses a dynamism toward the creation of an exclusive group that defines itself over against the others, is inimical to the notion of a baptized fellowship of equals. And it should go.

The Laity as Catalyst for Change

In thinking directly about the laity as a catalyst for change, we need to interweave two stories: one is the decline of the Catholic subculture and the impact of social changes, especially those of the fabled "sixties"; the other is the story of the reception of Vatican II. These two tales are often confused with each other. Conservative Catholics confuse the tales when they blame what they see as the decline of the church on a liberal "kidnapping" of the message of Vatican II, or even blame the council itself for a pollyannaish understanding of modernity. Liberals confuse them when they imagine that modernity and progress require the abandonment of tradition. Conservatives forget that traditionalism is the dead faith of the living. Liberals overlook the truth that tradition is the living faith of the dead. More traditional Catholics accuse progressives of having "thrown out the baby with the bath water," of having been unable to distinguish between the genuine reforms that needed to be made, and which Vatican II worked for, and the vitality of a popular culture and a devotional life whose loss has impoverished the Catholic imagination. Progressives respond often enough with the counterclaim that too many traditional Catholics are hankering after a golden age that never existed outside of movies such as *Going My Way*. Both have a point.

Two Tales

The Catholic subculture of the earlier part of the twentieth century lies in tatters in the first years of the twenty-first. The national network of thriving parishes staffed by numerous priests, each with its local school run by an order of nuns, is no more. Statues in churches, paraliturgies such as benediction, exposition of the sacrament, rosary, novenas, and so on are now apparently only minority tastes. If there are signs that some of them may be making a comeback, this is usually explained as residual or recidivist nostalgia. Parishes are increasingly likely to be staffed by a single priest or have no resident priest. Nuns are about as plentiful as two-dollar bills, soon perhaps to be as rare as three-dollar bills. And if there are a few thriving newer orders, the fact that they tend to prefer traditional floor-length habits and full wimples suggests, does it not, that they too are living in the past. "Vocations" to priesthood and religious life have shrunk to very low levels, and there are more priests in the United States today over ninety years of age than there are under thirty. Churches are being closed all over, particularly in the old urban centers of Catholicism, and Catholic schools survive, if at all, by taking in large numbers of non-Catholic children. Younger generation Catholics simply do not possess the cultural literacy of Catholicism, whether they are drawn to the church or not. Even those students most active in the church, though their prayer lives and commitment may put ours to shame, have no deep-seated loyalty to the community or its traditions. If the church disappoints them, they will go elsewhere. In sociological parlance, they are "voluntarist" Catholics—Catholics because they choose to be. They are rightly critical of a church bowed down under the scandal of sex abuse, but they will give of their time generously when their imaginations are captured. They will travel anywhere to see the pope, but they will sleep with their boyfriends and girlfriends along the way. And if the church disappoints them, they will walk away without a moment's regret.

The disappearance of the Catholic subculture is both a blessing and a curse. The principal problem it engenders is the decline of the role of imagination in religious life, with its attendant practices of prayer and the substitution of a broadly ethical or even existential understanding of religion as a search for meaning. As Robert Orsi, Harvard historian of popular Catholicism, makes so clear in his most recent book, *Between Heaven and Earth*, religion without the rich imaginative subculture becomes a poor tool for the storytelling that links this world and the world beyond. But there is an equally important benefit to the subculture's decline. While the church of the mid-twentieth century was marked by its laity's deference to the clergy and a mostly passive though rich devotional life, adult lay Catholics today are ready and willing to take more responsibility for the church and to speak out about its ills. This causes some pain, because the adult and educated status of the average Catholic today does not fit well into an institutional framework designed in and for an age when the laity were treated as children. But the pains are growing pains.

The tale of the council is one similarly mixed, and the versions you will hear are very dependent on the person proclaiming them. The problem with the legacy of the council is that it has not been properly "received." This is a technical theological term which suggests that teaching must be heard and put into practice for it to be truly significant. While it is possible to read the council documents in such a way that they largely reiterate the message of the past, the fact that the council was called at all, the fact that the council fathers staged a coup that involved the ouster of curial influence on their deliberations, and the fact that what is novel in the council's teaching is what we must attend to most closely all suggest that a reforming council is what we had in those years. This does not mean that any and every initiative subsequently taken in the name of the council was beyond reproach. The liturgical reforms were long overdue but were accompanied by overzealous efforts to remove all traces of the subculture from church buildings. But it does mean that all subsequent efforts to interpret the council need to be viewed through the lens of Vatican II's vision of the church as a community of the baptized, a people of God on a pilgrimage toward the heavenly city, in an open and dynamic relationship to the world, and not through the distorting lens of previous times in which the church as a perfect society sat in judgment on the secular world and every other religious tradition.

When we draw these two tales into relationship to each other, we can see how theological reception can be affected by cultural discomfort. At a superficial but informative level, we see it particularly clearly in the liberal and conservative responses to the sex-abuse scandal. Conservatives will tend to explain sex abuse as a result of an ethic of permissiveness and a rejection of the virtue of obedience, which they attribute to the council's kowtowing to the spirit of the times (read, "the '60s"). In its turn this will become a license for a selective appropriation of the council's teaching, so that the reassertion of papal infallibility and the hierarchical character of the church will overshadow, even smother, the equally significant attention to episcopal collegiality and the proclamation of the responsibilities of all the baptized. Liberals explain the sex-abuse scandal as an outgrowth of an unhealthy clericalism, in which the exclusively male and celibate priesthood policed itself about as badly as any other privileged and exclusive club. The truth of the matter is that the council did not provide the agenda for Opus Dei or for Call to Action, but it offers a challenge to both.

Where the Laity Are Today

The challenges and complexity of the postconciliar age can be seen clearly in a focus on the Catholic laity. They are, on the one hand, rather less likely to be weekly worshippers than they were forty years ago. They are much less likely to be frequent recipients of the sacrament of reconciliation or to attend paraliturgical worship services such as the rosary in common or the stations of the cross. On the other hand, the phenomenon of lay ministry in the church has grown astonishingly over the years since the council, as has the involvement of Catholics in ecclesiastical NGOs. To a degree, this is a response to the growing shortage of clergy and the need for the laity to take up the slack that this occasions. But it is surely also a sign of a thoroughly adult sense of personal accountability for the fortunes of the community, not just for the state of one's own soul. The American Catholic Church could not function today without the generosity and expertise of the 40,000 or so "lay ecclesial ministers." These are laypeople involved in full- or part-time, often paid, positions in the church. At one extreme, they administer parishes in the absence of a resident priest; at the other, they teach catechism to children. But all are essential to the work of the church. The American bishops have recognized the importance of lay ministry in a series of documents, the most recent of which was published in November 2005. In the next twenty years these lay ministers will come to outnumber the ranks of the clergy. With this demographic shift will inevitably come the pressure to scrutinize the nature of ministry and the differences, real and imagined, between priestly and lay ministry.

The existence of lay ecclesial ministers is indispensable to the church today, but the phenomenon also presents a challenge both to the understanding of the mission of the laity in general and to the idea of sacred orders. On the one hand, the very importance of lay ecclesial ministry can distract the church's attention from the indispensable ministry to the world which the whole baptized people are called to undertake. And on the other, the phenomenon of full-time lay employees in work formerly done by priests or perhaps religious sisters challenges us to ask about the precise difference between someone "ordained" to serve the church and someone clearly called but without the formal designation of ordination. Let us pursue both these points a little further.

When the council spoke of the "essentially secular" character of the laity it was not making a derogatory comment intended to exclude them from responsible voice inside the church, though it may unintentionally have provided ammunition for those who wish to do exactly that, if only by its choice of the word "secular." The important point the council fathers were making was that the first responsibility of baptized Christians is to the mission of the church to the world. Much of Vatican II, especially the documents on the church in the modern world, on religious freedom, and even on relations with other religions, establishes an entirely refreshing—might one even say "new"?—relationship between the Catholic Church and the human community beyond it, both religious and secular. This mission, the task to which God calls the church, is the principal responsibility of the baptized. "Secular," then, is not meant to imply "not sacred," which is why the word was a poor choice, but rather "worldly" in the best sense of the word. Of course, "worldly" itself is open to misunderstanding, when it is thought of in the sense that the values of the world are uncritically absorbed. Rather, "worldly" should be understood in the sense that the laity are at home in the world which God created and God loves—the place that is our home, the place where all of us are called to work out our salvations. In other words, I suppose one could say, the laity are called to be "secular" in exactly the same sense that Jesus of Nazareth was secular, a layperson with a mission from God.

Given the essentially secular character of the laity, then, what exactly are we to make of those who serve the church as lay ecclesial ministers? The documents of Vatican II, which set the scene for this development without formally establishing it or perhaps imagining how quickly it would come to be indispensable to the church, mostly see lay ministers as those who fill a gap left by a shortage of priests. While Vatican II thought the shortage was most likely to occur in what they called missionary situations, we know today that the problem is becoming equally acute in Europe and North America. This vision of lay ministry within the church has been described as "the apostolate of the second string." This very telling term suggests that if and when ordained clergy become plentiful again, the laity will be thanked and returned to the bench to await the next emergency. It is certainly true that Vatican II's discussion of the lay role in ministries with the faith community often gives the impression that they are a temporary expedient. However, what if we are never going to see the rise in traditional vocations again? What if God is working something wonderful through the decline in the ranks of the traditional ordained ministry? If this is even a possibility, and it would be rash to conclude that the Holy Spirit cannot work in this way, then we may need to raise a wholly different set of questions.

As lay ministry increases in importance and is matched by a decline in the number of traditional clergy, questions will be asked about the sacrament of orders. Indeed, this has already begun with the increased focus in pastoral and sacramental theology on the relationship between baptism and mission. Baptism is not merely a sacrament of initiation; it is entry into a missioned community. Most of the baptized have as their mission to be other Christs in the world. Many, however, are called to work within the community of faith. What exactly is the difference between ordained ministry and that of others? The answer is not to point to celibacy or the exclusively male priesthood. Traditionally, the response is to assert that ordination etches an indelible mark or "character" on the soul, making the ordained minister somehow ontologically different from those not ordained. But increasingly this language of "substantial ontological change" is being challenged by the parallel notion of "relational ontological change." That is, what happens in ordination is that the relationship of the ordinand to the community undergoes radical change. This shift in thinking has many consequences, not the least that the change envisaged here is precisely similar in kind, if not always in degree, to the change effected in one who becomes a parish administrator or a youth minister or a catechist. And so we might want to venture two claims at this point. First, we can see that a theology of orders has overshadowed the theology of baptism for much of the history of the church, especially since the language of substantial ontological change came into prominence in the Middle Ages. This imbalance needs to be corrected by an insistence that it is in baptism that we become a new creation, not in ordination. Second, we can also see that the most helpful way of distinguishing callings in the church is not the traditional one of "clergy" and "laity," since it cannot absorb the category of lay ecclesial ministry. Rather, the best distinction is between ministry in the church and ministry to the world. Taken together, these two observations elevate the role of what we have traditionally known as the laity, just as they put "ordained" ministry in its place as one vocation among others. We will discuss this set of issues at more length in chapter 4.

It is sad that church leaders have not yet reached this point in their reflections, and are inclined to be much more on the defensive, shoring up old ways as if they were the only ones possible. In a brave address given to the priests of the Milwaukee archdiocese, Fr. Bryan Massingale, a priest of the diocese who teaches ethics at Marquette University, proposes a model of priestly ministry for today as hospice care. The present form of the institutional church is dying, he says, and it has to be helped to face up to its own mortality, while at the same time trying to maintain a quality of life, all while we await the wonderful transforming work of the Spirit, who will bring new life out of the old. If Massingale is right, then our church leaders are simply in denial. There is no other explanation for the crisis in ministry being answered solely by prayers for traditional vocations and sets of rules to insist on the rigid separation between the roles of the ordained and the laity. Hope for the future needs to be accompanied by a little courage and imagination. As Massingale would surely agree, awaiting the transforming work of the Spirit should be accompanied by a little preparing the way of the Lord.

Bibliographical Note

The discussions of the early history of the laity and the fortunes of the laity at Vatican II can be reviewed in more detail in the early chapters of my book *The Liberation of the Laity: In Search of an Accountable Church* (New York: Continuum, 2003). A much fuller treatment of the role of laity in ministry can be found in Edward P. Hahnenberg's fine book *Ministries: A Relational Approach* (New York: Crossroad, 2003). The U.S. Catholic bishops have recently published a new document on lay ministry, *Co-Workers in the Vineyard of the Lord* (Washington, D.C.: United States Conference of Catholic Bishops, 2006). The text of this document is available online at http://www.usccb.org/laity/laymin/. You can read Bryan Massingale's stirring words, "See, I Am Doing Something New!" at http://www.jknirp.com/massin.htm.

Discussion Questions

1. Can you come up with a definition of "lay" that does not use negatives and that does not apply equally to the ordained? If not, what does this say about the content of the term "lay"?
2. What would it mean for a parish or diocese if we abandoned the terms "priests" and "laypeople" and talked of "different ministries"? Specifically, what would it mean for the community of faith for all persons to think of themselves as possessing some kind of mission or ministry?
3. In your local parish faith community, how are lay ministers perceived, relative to the ordained and relative to the regular laity? Are they thought of as lay leaders, or as emergency workers in a shortage of priests, "the apostolate of the second string," or what?
4. How might we restore a sense in the church of baptism as entry into a priestly mission?

Chapter Three

WHAT IS SO IMPORTANT ABOUT ACCOUNTABILITY?

When you have raised children, or even if you have just been around them as a favorite uncle or a teacher, you know something about their slow progress toward becoming adults. At first you cuddle them through their early years. Then, by stages, a little discipline enters the mix. The challenge is to get the mix right as the years go by, blending age-appropriate demonstrations of love and discipline. If you are both wise and a little lucky, then you will see the beauty of the young adult emerging from the cocoon of adolescent self-absorption. Your child has grown to see that responsibility and freedom in healthy balance are the stuff of which adulthood is made. You can breathe a sigh of relief, perhaps mixed with a little sadness. The kids are off into the world, to face its challenges. They won't always get it right, but out on their own they will do pretty well. Maybe the parents will be turned to for advice from time to time, but on the whole it is now their world and their task.

The American Catholic Church today looks a lot like a family in which the parents are clinging desperately to the illusion that their children are still infants. How else would we describe a situation in which every decision is a parental responsibility and the children have no say? What other conclusion could we come to about a church in which there is no requirement that the bishops ever seek advice from the people and in which by definition the people cannot have any executive authority or any formal responsibilities for leadership? If a family behaved that way when the children were way beyond childhood, then we would think there was something wrong, probably something wrong with the parents. And we would probably not be surprised to see the children flee the nest.

The image of parent and children has little value for interpreting the relationship between the American bishops and the Catholic people. True it helps us to see how clericalist bishops and a few lay enablers are responsible for a dysfunctional ecclesiastical family. Beyond that it doesn't help because the image is plain wrong. Laypeople are not children of the bishops; they, like the bishops, are children of the Lord, and we are all in this together. To understand the church we have to get past distinctions between the ordained and the laity and concentrate instead on the unity and equality that comes with baptism. In baptism we become a new creation and we share in the priesthood of Christ. Everything else is secondary. Everything else about the church has come about as the priestly people has sought to find ways to be more effective as the loving presence of Christ in the world. Everything else about the church is supposed to help this task or mission that Christ has given us. If it helps, keep it. If not, discard it. Of course, this discernment process is not easy, but that is why the Holy Spirit was promised to the church—to help the church remain faithful to its purpose. Popes and bishops are guided by the Spirit in their teaching, and the whole faithful people is guided in its prayerful practice by exactly the same Spirit. Together, over history, we discern how best to remain faithful.

The family metaphor and the story of growth into adulthood is much more helpful in thinking about the relationship between God and the church. It is the church and not just the laity that has to grow up. Of course, God is not a neurotic parent who cannot abide the thought that the children will mature and stand on their own feet. Quite the contrary. God wants above all that human beings have the freedom in which their growth in love for one another and for God becomes possible. The parent who binds the child to the parental apron strings, who insists on dependency, is only assuring that the love that is returned will be less than it might be. There is no true love without freedom. The love that is constrained is not love. And "growing up" means growing more like God because it means growing in the capacity to love. The more we can love, the more like God we are. But love requires freedom and responsibility. The freer and more responsible we are, the more like God we are. Thus a faith community that does not encourage true freedom and that therefore makes responsibility an illusion is effectively preventing itself from growing more like God. This is quite a judgment on a dysfunctional church.

To explore the value of this metaphor of maturation for the life of the church today we need to think about four things. First, we need to be clear what we mean when we talk about accountability, credibility, and authority, and their relationship to one another. Second, we shall then be able to see that the best model we have for accountability in the fullest sense of the word is the Trinity itself. So we will have to think some about what the life of God might be like, and then, third, go on to see if it suggests things to us about the way the life of the church ought to be. Fourth, we'll test what we have discovered by applying it to the important topic of authority in the church and the authority of the church.

Accountability and Credibility

At the heart of religions of all kinds is the conviction that we are neither our own explanation nor our reason for living. It would seem a logical consequence of this belief, wouldn't it, that a sense of accountability would permeate the practice of Christian living? If we owe all we have and are to something beyond ourselves, then we surely have a responsibility beyond ourselves. Accountability is the public face of responsibility, illustrated in our willingness to submit our actions to the judgment of others. It follows directly from the recognition that the human being is not in the first instance an individual equipped with inalienable rights, but rather a member of a community whose rights are always proportionate to the rights of others. It is best illustrated in the family (which, not entirely irrelevantly, is often referred to by pastoral theologians as "the domestic church"). Ideally speaking, a family is a community marked by unconditional love of its members for one another, in which this love is directed outward to the world that family members will eventually make their own. The family is thus both the domestic church and a school of humanity. Most families, of course, do not fully live up to these high ideals, but the fulfillment of these ideals is surely what families are actually *for*. And in the family that is striving to be what a family should be, full accountability of all family members to one another is an ideal that is not entirely beyond reach. Depending on the level of maturity of the family member, the mixture of freedom and responsibility varies, but two characteristics are constant. First, all, including the most senior members of the family, are accountable to all the others. Second, this accountability is not best understood as accountability of children to parents and parents to children, but rather as accountability of each individual to the family understood as a whole.

There are at least three different senses of the term "accountability." First, there is the very limited understanding of accountability as the obedience of those with lesser positions in the family or community to those with more senior or "higher" positions. In familial terms, this would be evident in the unfashionable and even discredited vision of the Victorian family, where the stern *pater familias* is rarely seen, and then only to give orders. Beyond this impoverished understanding of accountability there are two richer applications. One is the "lower" accountability of all family or community members to one another. Here we are no longer talking about obedience but about a sense of responsibility to and for one another. The other or "higher" accountability is the deeper mutuality and web of loving relationships which is consistent with the lower accountability and could not exist without it, but which goes far beyond it. Trust, love, and mutuality in a successful family transcend even the genuinely reciprocal responsibility that marks the lower accountability. And the model for this is the mutuality of God and Israel in the Hebrew covenant. There, God and Israel make promises to each other, but they are only the public face of an enduring love.

One of the most frequently expressed criticisms of the Catholic Church in the last few years, stemming from the level of scrutiny occasioned by the scandal of clerical sexual abuse of minors, is that the practice of accountability is poor. This observation is accurate but may miss some of the complexity of the problem by failing to distinguish between the different senses or levels of accountability. In today's church, in fact, accountability is primarily understood in the first, impoverished sense of obedience to higher authority. Accountability operates only in one direction, upward, so that laity are accountable to their pastors, clergy are accountable to bishops, and bishops to the pope. This could be fairly simply solved by instituting the kinds of structures that most human communities would consider healthy and have laypeople periodically do performance reviews of their clergy, clergy of their bishops, and bishops of the pope. Indeed, this would be an enormously healthy step for the church to take. We would then at least be on the verge of commitment to a genuine application of the lower accountability, but we would still be in danger of missing the deeper values. This contractual accountability might be contrasted fruitfully with a covenantal accountability that we have already discussed in the case of family but that may have its clearest human expression in the marital relationship. Accountability in this sense is a dimension of love, and it is buttressed with the values of openness, trust, and fundamental equality, which are important in most understandings of marriage.

Before we relate the question of accountability to how we understand the church, we should say a thing or two about the relationship between accountability and credibility, and we can do this by returning to the familial metaphor one more time. How often have those of us who are parents of adolescents found ourselves exclaiming, "If you want to be treated like an adult, behave like an adult!" Credibility is directly proportional to the level of practice of accountability. But whereas accountability is a practice for which, in the last analysis, we as individuals are responsible, credibility is something we acquire in the eyes of others through the transparency of our practice of accountability. Respect must be earned. It should never be extended to a person simply because of her or his status, and while respect can pertain to particular roles, that of parent, for example, it should not be afforded to the parent merely because he or she is a parent. Of course, younger children may not have developed the discernment to know when to give and when to withhold respect, but that soon changes. Children rapidly learn to discern dishonesty, whether demonstrated by parents, teachers, or peers. Respect follows from the credibility that is based on the public practice of accountability. Anything else simply enables dysfunctional behavior.

The Church and the Triune God

One of the great ironies of the Catholic Church is that while it is devoted to a Trinitarian God it has resolutely adopted a hierarchical structure. One would think, on the face of it, that the ecclesial structure that God would want for the church would be one that took the hint from God's nature about the superiority of trinitarianism over hierarchical stratification. Just as the call to Christian discipleship should suggest to us a life lived according to the values and choices of Jesus of Nazareth, so you would think that the church of God would reflect what seems to be the divine preference for relationship. What would happen if we modeled the church on the life of God instead of on the structures of the Roman Empire or the Ford Motor Company? One would think that it would be a good thing. It would certainly seem that the efforts at Vatican II and beyond to build a communion ecclesiology represented steps in this direction, yet so much in Catholicism remains undeniably hierarchical. In fact it may not be too outrageous a statement to say that wherever hierarchy has been represented in the church's history as the fundamental structure of the church, the church has been envisaged in a manner antithetical to that community of persons which God's inner nature so clearly tells us is the preferred form of social life. When Vatican II made the hierarchical structure of the church secondary to understanding the church as the People of God, it took a giant step toward growing closer to God. Hierarchy does not reflect the divine life; mutuality does.

We Christians believe in a Trinitarian God, that is, that God is a communion of persons. Of course, there is not a lot we can say about what the inner life of God is like, but there are a few illuminating things we can say if indeed it is true, as we believe, that the one God is a communion of three persons. First and most important, while there is differentiation among the three persons of the Godhead, there are no ranks. All are equally and fully God, despite the distinctions that are traditionally asserted in the terminology of Father, Son, and Spirit or somewhat differently claimed in the language of Creator, Redeemer, and Sanctifier. Each is God; each is the whole God; each is equally God. Any image that the human imagination can come up with to represent the Trinity must, if it is to be acceptable, respect this equality. Second, the radical equality of the three persons of the Trinity does not extinguish their difference. Third, the difference that each expresses is something we encounter, as human beings, only in their relationship to our salvation, in what theologians call the "economic" Trinity. What these differences mean within the divine life is not for us to know, though Christians throughout history, especially the great mystics, have tried to come up with images that express something of the mystery. In any case, we surely know that the persons of the Trinity are differentiated in terms of what we might call divine mission or ministry. In plain language, they have different responsibilities in the plan of salvation. This is where we encounter the persons of the Trinity, in their relation to our salvation, in their different missions. But it is part of Christian faith that the way we encounter God is consistent with the inner life of God, if only because the self-revelation of God cannot be fraudulent or misleading. We can then confidently assert that the equality with which Father, Son, and Spirit pursue their different missions cannot stand in contradiction to their life, which must itself be one of mutuality and interrelationship of equality within difference.

The inner life of the Trinity is the preeminent model for us of that higher accountability we have already touched on as the real issue for the church. The three persons of the Trinity do not have to explain their actions to one another. Their lower accountability is subsumed in the higher accountability of a relationship of total openness and perfect equality. The language of the ancient Cappadocian fathers of the church, as they searched for an image to envision the Trinity, is particularly helpful here. To them, the three persons are engaged in *perichoresis*, that is, in a divinely and intricately interwoven dance formation. This is no heavenly hip-hop, rave, or stomp. They are *intertwined* with one another. Picture talented quick-step dancers or *aficionados* of the tango. There is no way that they can successfully accomplish their mission without complete openness to and trust in one another. They will fall over and lose their dignity. Or think of the accountability of trapeze artists for one another. One slip and they might die. Success requires the trust that comes with total accountability. If this is the model for divine mutuality and Trinitarian structure, then perhaps the church should move more in that same direction. It is surely a salutary warning against any attempt to idealize church structures that, in searching for human metaphors to help us think about God, the hierarchical structure of the church does not immediately spring to mind.

Accountability in the Church

These perhaps presumptuous reflections on the divine life should suggest how impoverished our ecclesial understandings of accountability tend to be. The everyday legalistic language about accountability certainly has its place, particularly after the fiasco of episcopal failures of leadership in the wake of the sexual abuse scandal. But in the end all this is not much more than nursery accountability. Do what you say you will do, be responsible, be ready to explain your actions and take the consequences, and so on. It is not unimportant, but it is only the first step toward true adult accountability. Think again of the ballroom dancers who cannot do what they do without total trust in one another and practiced coordination. Their accountability has been bred into their bones. Perhaps we could venture further still, to the mutual eros and agape of accountability that we find in human life most commonly in marriage, and that is in itself a pale shadow of the eros and agape of the divine life.

Pale shadow it may be, but when it is practiced it makes us more like God.

If the church is truly to practice accountability in the fullest sense of the word, then both its polity and its culture must manifest total mutuality. While there is a hierarchical structure to orders in the church, indicating levels of responsibility to serve, it should never be interpreted in terms of power, still less of levels of holiness attached to strata of power, if the church is truly to be the church of God. Of course, there are differences in the mission of people in the church as they place their particular gifts at the service of the church. Some people will take up leadership positions, and leadership sometimes involves the exercise of authority, even if that is often a confession of failure. But the model for leaders in the church cannot be the stern Victorian parental image of a God who distantly corrects and sometimes chastises. That is the wrong image of God, and therefore of God's church. We are invited into the divine life. We are called to the same loving interrelatedness that the Trinity is, and our leaders— while their mission is to lead—should be held to the same standards of fundamental equality as the divine life itself exemplifies. To put it most directly, if God is fundamentally interpersonal how can the church be anything else?

The problem of lack of accountability in the church is in the last analysis, therefore, not that the appropriate two-way openness of a healthy institution is lacking—though this *is* lacking in the church and it is something that needs to be addressed—but that the church has placed such organizational paraphernalia ahead of a fundamental reality that is constantly in danger of being forgotten. We can make the point in the categories of personal and structural sin. When a bishop hides his personal failings behind the walls of clerical culture, he is guilty of personal sin. This sin is enabled by the structural sin of clericalism. But this structural sin is in its turn a product of profound theological amnesia, of a far greater sin in which pride, power, and status have led the church too often into the error of thinking that its hierarchical structure is its essence. Its essence, as Vatican II has taught us, is relationship, interrelatedness, or *communio*. *Lumen Gentium*'s chapter on "the people of God," remember, comes before the chapter on hierarchy. The way forward for the church must then be to reform its structures so that it is clearly seen to be a community of complete accountability, closer in consequence to the triune God whom it exists to serve.

If it is true that this Trinitarian accountability is something to which the church is called, then the church must demonstrate the characteristics of an open society. But the institutions of the Catholic Church of today too often perpetuate secrecy and seem to be incapable of seeing any virtue in a measure of democracy within the church. Indeed, it is really extraordinary that although the church over the centuries has continually acquired at least some of the characteristics of the political culture in which it has existed, that process seemed to stop in the years after the Council of Trent. In the early years of a new millennium, then, the political structures of Catholicism remain a curious blend of Roman imperial practices and the trappings of medieval monarchy. As Charles Taylor pointed out in his distinguished Marianist lecture a few years ago, the virtues of the Enlightenment and of modernity—justice, equality, free speech, and so on—are qualities that the church had to learn from secular society because it could not have found the resources in itself to discover them. Truly, those virtues have been incorporated into much of the wise teaching that the Catholic Church has offered the world at least since the time of Leo XIII but, as has so often been pointed out, rarely if ever employed in the internal life of the church.

Many commentators have observed that in the American church at least, the grassroots is pretty healthy. With the involvement of large numbers of lay ministers in our communities of faith, there is vibrancy to the best of our parishes that the shortage of ordained ministers apparently does not spoil. Indeed, at least in the near term, this shortage of ordained ministers may be precisely what has reminded the church of the apostolicity of the lay vocation. In the days of Arianism, many bishops weakened in their resolve and failed in their responsibility for leadership. The laity stepped in, not by assuming the leadership that bishops had abandoned, but in maintaining the practice of their faith despite poor leadership. Today, it seems, the realities of *communio* are to be found, if anywhere, in the religious life of the local faith community. And sadly, that *communio* often exists despite and not because of the leadership in the church.

While the church today is not openly dealing with a threat of heresy, it is in crisis. This crisis is occasioned by a fundamental misconception of what is central to the church. Despite the rhetoric of communion ecclesiology that the teachings of Vatican II more or less mandated, the Roman restorationism of the past quarter of a century has returned us institutionally to where we were before Vatican II. That is a place in which the responsibility of the community to mirror the relationality of the divine life has been overwhelmed by the *wholly* human predilection for rules, regulations, buildings, status, power over others, secrecy, silence, ambition, and expediency. None of this is from God. The German Lutheran theologian Dorothee Soelle did not mince her words when she described this kind of phenomenon as "necrophilia." She had a point. The church thrives by sharing in the life of God through the body and blood of Christ, not through the dead stuff of institutional bureaucracy.

Authority and Democratization:
A Test Case for the Higher Accountability

The scandal of sexual abuse has reinvigorated calls in the American Catholic Church for greater democratization, especially for the role of a lay voice in financial affairs, in pastoral councils, and in the selection of pastors and bishops. More longstanding debates, at least in the church of the northern hemisphere, over sexual ethics and bioethical concerns, over the celibacy of the clergy and the ordination of women, also implicitly testify to the same concerns. The institutional response to much, if not all, of this turmoil has been to label it "dissent," and more conservative Catholics have declared these kinds of concerns to be *ipso facto* evidence of lack of fidelity to the church.

It is obvious that there needs to be a lay voice in dealing with the scandal of sex abuse, but that is an issue we will turn to in chapter 5. The underlying issues to be considered in this chapter should not, however, be allowed to hide the fact that, as almost always in the church, the battleground for accountability and adulthood starts, if it does not end, in the parish. Relations between pastors and people are for the most part not carried out along the patriarchal or paternalistic lines so common in the past. Where the old patterns still exist, however, as they do in some churches in every diocese, they must simply be stamped out. Here the people have much more real power than the local bishop, and they must use it. Financial councils should exist in every parish, and the people cannot allow the pastor to sidestep or ignore them. Pastoral councils should be insisted upon. And when the pastor has decided, as not a few seem to have done, to turn the clock back and outlaw female altar servers or sneak pieces of the Latin Mass back into the vernacular form, or try subtly to return the liturgy to the way it was before Vatican II, he must simply be told by the lay leadership of the parish that this is plainly unacceptable. The issue here is not a matter of taste. Vatican II's liturgical changes were intended to stress the fact that the liturgy is the work of the whole gathered community, not that of the priest alone. Moreover, learning to respond in this way is not a school of dissent but a school of accountability, for both people and pastor.

It is important for liberal and conservative Catholics alike to understand that the debate over authority and democratization is not in the end about political structures in the institution, but about whether the church is a divine or a human reality. Of course, it is both human and divine, but the insistence on unthinking obedience to a hierarchically structured polity is the reduction of the church to a purely human reality. Curiously enough, it is the liberal call for more voice for all that is seeking to bring the church closer to the divine life, and therefore working for its holiness. Liberals who stop at a simple critique of the dysfunctional elements of our present church structures are playing into the hands of the institution by accepting the rules of the game as the institution understands them. "The hierarchy" is God-given, conservative voices will say. "The hierarchy" is a human element in the church and hence changeable, liberals might counter. The truth is that good order in the church *is* God-given, but it is a structure of openness, accountability, and holiness patterned on the divine life, not the pyramid of power that has bedeviled the church since the Middle Ages. The good order of the church is not necessarily tied to any particular polity—not to that of imperialism or autocratic monarchy or benevolent despotism. The Trinitarian model we have explored does not necessarily mandate democracy either, but it certainly suggests a strong preference for collaborative engagement with the common tasks of Christian mission.

"Authority" is a characteristic of the whole church, insofar as it is holy/accountable/open based on the pattern of the divine life. The mission of different individuals in the church may express that authority of the whole church in different ways, but it is in virtue of sharing in the authority of the whole church that a bishop or a prophet can claim authority. This approach to authority, for example, lies behind the understanding of papal infallibility as the pope expressing what "has always been the faith of the Church," not deriving or determining interpretations of doctrine on his own authority. The collective authority of the bishops and the practical infallibility of the *sensus fidelium* (the sense of the faithful) are similarly envisaged.

The fundamental problem of authority in the church in the present day is not that this or that pope is perceived by some to exceed his authority, or that liberal laity are dissenters, or that episcopal collegiality is underexercised. The deepest problem is that the church has lost authority in a world that needs its leadership so much, because it has lost credibility. And loss of credibility, in its turn, must be put down to a public failure to be a fully open, accountable community. What the world sees is inevitably the failures in lower accountability, with poor episcopal leadership in the sex-abuse scandal as the primary example in North America in recent times. In the nineteenth century, the racism of the American Catholic Church might have been the public face of lack of accountability. But we in the community of faith can come to understand that such failures in accountability are attributable to our failures in that higher accountability. If we were ready to recognize that the life of the church must seek to mirror the divine life, the lower accountability would mostly take care of itself. Until we take this step, we will continue to be embroiled in sterile debates about who is dissenting from what.

Bibliographical Note

The theology of the relationship between the Trinity and church order is most effectively presented by Miroslav Volf in *After Our Likeness: The Church as the Image of the Trinity* (Grand Rapids: Eerdmans, 1997). Charles Taylor's fascinating explanation of what the church owes to secular thought is available in very readable form in *A Catholic Modernity?* (New York: Oxford, 1999). Those who would like to explore the idea of "communion ecclesiology" in more detail can do so in Dennis Doyle's book, *Communion Ecclesiology: Visions and Versions* (Maryknoll, N.Y.: Orbis Books, 2000).

Discussion Questions

1. Can any light be shed on the dynamics of the parish or diocese by using the parent/child metaphor? Do the clergy see themselves as having parental responsibilities? Do the laity prefer to be treated like children?
2. Vatican II called on laypeople to speak up for the good of the church. How often does this happen in the local community of faith? What are the consequences?
3. Does the fact that the Trinitarian God is not hierarchical have any lessons to teach us about church structures?
4. What would be the plusses and minuses of introducing a measure of democracy into church practice? Where might it be useful? Where might it be counterproductive?

Chapter Four

ACCOUNTABILITY AND THE LAITY: WHAT'S THE POINT?

In all the talk about accountability in the church, what are the particular responsibilities of the laity? Our challenge in this chapter is to think this through, to explore the ways in which accountability figures in lay life and the promise that the lay experience of accountability may hold for the church as a whole. What are the hurdles that laypeople face in taking responsibility for their church? What are the warrants for taking responsibility? And what are some of the forms that this responsibility should take? Most of us are adults who have a measure of responsibility in our everyday lives, whether for raising children, taking care of elderly parents, practicing complex brain surgery, or something in between. But by and large, laypeople do not exercise responsibility for the church, beyond the financial demands that are made upon us. This situation is irrefutable, and it is a product of many centuries of neglect of the lay role in the church. But had it not been so, if even a couple of generations of mid-twentieth century lay Catholics had not been asleep in the pews, fewer predator priests would have had their way with so many children.

The Laity: Experts in Accountability

Every sector of the church has its particular strengths; everyone has something to contribute. Bishops have as their particular responsibility the unity of the church, whether the universal church that is the special concern of the bishop of Rome, or the local church in any given diocese. Priests must preside at worship and see to the unity of their own local community. Theologians, whether bishops, priests, or laypeople, must study the tradition and teach in ways that keep faith strong in changing times. Laypeople bring many gifts to the community, but right now the most important contribution that laypeople as laypeople have to offer the church is the testimony to the value of personal accountability. Right now, this may be the prophetic dimension of lay life.

In everything they do, laypeople are accountable. In our work lives we are accountable to employers, clients, students, patients, those who work for us. But more important, in our personal lives most of us are accountable to partners, spouses, children, extended family. If we do not balance our checkbooks, terrible things can happen. If we do not pay our mortgage, it can get even worse. If we are irresponsible in our use of alcohol, or take to drugs, or seek sexual intimacy outside our domestic frameworks, we put our very lives in jeopardy, offer bad example to our children, and cause pain to those we love. In the end, except perhaps for the truly wealthy among us, laypeople live less secure lives than the clergy. Short of actual criminal activity, clerical futures are assured in ways that ours are not. As things stand in the church at the present time, this level of security is a reasonable gift to give a celibate clergy. But it carries with it the challenge of being accountable to others. Being responsible to yourself alone is so much more difficult.

It is clear that the clerical lifestyle in the church is morally unaccountable, which is not at all to say that the clergy are any less moral than laypeople. Indeed, it may be that because moral accountability is not demanded of the clergy, particularly the diocesan clergy, the great majority who live morally exemplary lives are to be commended for their practices. It is so much harder to be accountable to yourself for your choices than it is to know that your spouse is there to call you to account. Poor moral choices are so much easier to make when no one else is apparently going to know or care. It doesn't matter whether we are talking about financial decisions, sexual morality, alcohol abuse, drugs, or what have you. The lives of the clergy are made more difficult by their being alone. And if this leads smoothly into an argument against mandatory celibacy, at least it is not the usual one. Many parochial clergy thrive under the law of celibacy, though for a lot of them it is a cross bravely borne for the sake of the priesthood, not a conscious preference for a life alone. Indeed, it is not at all clear that someone to whom a lifelong partnership with another human being would be alarming or inimical is likely to make a good priest. The usual argument for a celibate clergy is that it provides for a life of more single-minded generosity than is possible in married life, where there are always competing claims on our attention. The truth of the matter is that celibacy *can* work in such a way, perhaps should, but in practice is at least as likely to lead to self-involvement and frequently to the irresponsibility that arises from the absence of accountability to a concrete "other." The point is not that many priests would be better priests if they had more sex without guilt or needed to pay a mortgage or to budget for orthodontist's bills. But it is quite true that many of their lives would be more fruitful and more moral if their personal choices had to be made in the context of family or spousal obligations. Marriage is neither paradise nor a panacea. But it is a wonderful school of accountability.

This set of observations about the practicalities of accountability now needs to be raised to another level. This occurs when we realize that lives built around professional and domestic obligations, whether those of partnered or single people, with or without children, say something essential about human life. The human person is from the first moment of life intended by God to be embraced by a loving community within which she or he will come to be the person one is. No community, no truly formed individual. Spirituality is nothing more or less than life lived intentionally, and for Christians that means life lived in the light of God's creative will. We are born to be together, not to be alone. And accountability is what keeps us together, just as much and sometimes more than the purely romantic dimensions of love. Love is a blend of eros and agape. Too often the church talks as if eros is blind sexual desire and agape is laudable self-sacrifice. Some truth here, but lay life "marries" the two (no pun intended). Laypeople know that the two are closely intertwined, and that the fullest meaning of agape is not self-sacrifice but accountability.

Laypeople and clergy are not in fact divided by this issue of accountability, since there are many laypeople living the single life, by choice or accident, for whom many of the challenges of accountability are shared with celibate clergy. And even now there are a few married Catholic priests who know firsthand the immediate accountability that goes with spousal and familial obligations. But on the whole at the present moment, before the law of clerical celibacy is changed, as will surely come to pass, laypeople as a matter of fact are distinguished from clergy by the more direct accountability that goes with lack of ultimate security and the presence of domestic responsibilities. This is a good thing for the church, for now. Its presence in lay life is one of the reasons why laypeople have been shocked by the crisis of leadership revealed in the scandal of sexual abuse. The abusers are sick and psychologically immature people who have preyed on the innocent. But the enablers are supposedly our leaders in the faith, who have far too often given evidence of irresponsible inattention to accountability, both for their own actions and those of the perpetrators. It is because we laypeople know the discipline of accountability and are aware, perhaps in our own lives, of the price that we can pay for lapses in that accountability that we have to insist on it in our church. We are the experts in accountability. We are the teachers. We need to teach. Unfortunately, the church is short on classrooms and educational institutes in which we all can learn from the collective wisdom of lay experience.

The Difficulty of Taking Responsibility

In trying as laypeople to take responsibility for our church we immediately come face to face with the fact that there are no formal structures or avenues through which the lay voice can be articulated.

We do not have the synodal structure of the Episcopalian or Lutheran traditions, nor the lay governance structures of Presbyterianism. Canon law certainly provides for diocesan synods in which the lay voice would be heard, but there is no mandate that bishops must hold such events, nor is there any clarity about how the lay voice in these synods should be chosen. Consequently, lay voices for change are commonly forced into forming what we might call ecclesiastical NGOs, such as Call to Action or Voice of the Faithful. Their conservative counterparts, such as Catholics United for the Faith or Faithful Voice, intent on resisting change, must do the same. This situation is much less healthy than would be one in which the various points of view represented across the spectrum of church opinion met and challenged one another in a kind of public forum internal to the faith community. It was this problem that the late Cardinal Joseph Bernardin of Chicago was trying to address with his "Common Ground Initiative," and although it continues to some degree, the church as a whole seems to have grown more polarized, not less, in the years since his death.

If what makes it so hard to take responsibility in the church is the lack of formal structures through which the lay voice can be heard, then we need to ask why this is so. The short answer is that the church is a site of structural oppression, but the term "structural oppression" has to be handled very carefully, lest it be simply dismissed as a further contribution to polarization. "Structural oppression" refers to the ways in which any society or community can have its options limited or its freedoms circumscribed by structures within its particular culture, even and perhaps especially structures that many are unaware of and that most have no direct investment in perpetuating. So this is not a matter of bishops oppressing the rest of us or clergy oppressing laypeople. The villains are not bishops or clerics, but structures. The humanity of bishops is placed as much under threat in a structurally oppressive church as is the humanity of the wealthy in a class-polarized society, or that of slave owners in a slave society. Indeed, the sinners are all of us, clergy and laity, who live without protest in such an oppressed condition. Breaking out of such a situation occurs when consciousness is raised among the oppressed class to the fact of their oppression, and movement for change is initiated. In our church the sex-abuse scandal has been the catalyst for this conscientization, because it has led us beyond the scandal to a new critical awareness of our ecclesial reality. Hence come the calls for a reconsideration of issues of authority, governance, and accountability, through which the laity are attempting to reclaim their rightful roles as responsible agents in the church, not merely passive subjects.

It is clear that structural oppression affects all of us, and we have to face the fact that the primary form it takes is the clerical stranglehold on leadership in the church. It is a principal point of the argument of this book that the exclusion of lay experience from leadership and decision making impoverishes the whole church, but it is the laity who feel the oppressive structures most directly. So, at this moment in the church it is certainly the case that many theologically trained Catholics are laypeople, but none of them has any formal role in teaching. It is beyond dispute that the wisdom and experience of laypeople in issues of marriage and family simply overwhelms whatever the clergy may know, yet laypeople have no say in the formation of ethical teaching on these issues. Perhaps more important still, there is no way for the situation to change without those in positions of power—the clergy and especially the bishops—marginalizing their own privileged position, since laypeople have no formal way of influencing church structures. And finally, if we admit that there will always be some who will have the gift of leadership, though most do not (and who would disagree with this?), it is very difficult to explain how the gift of leadership coincides so completely with the commitment to a celibate life within the ranks of a clerical caste.

Using the language of structural oppression raises for some people the specter of liberation theology. Liberation theology gets bad press in the church because it challenges structural oppression. But in the end, liberation theologians have simply accepted that the God of freedom who brought the slaves out of Egypt and made them into God's people and the Christ who proclaimed the priority of the Spirit of God over the letter of the law call all of us to our true humanity and personhood under the sign of the cross and resurrection. God in Jesus Christ expresses a "preferential option" for the marginalized. This option is not exhausted in the corporal works of mercy, important as they are. It reaches its high point in a call for changed consciousness, change that will not only demonstrate social and political consequences but that will also primarily be validated in the just society envisaged in the message of the prophets and the teaching of Jesus. Any structures that impede the fullness of responsible human flourishing in the world, which is our home, are sinful and need to be swept aside. Liberation theologians love the church, but they feel its pain too, and they locate its sickness often enough in just those structures that seem to interfere with the freedom of the Spirit to endow whomsoever the Spirit wishes with gifts for the good of the church.

The challenge, evidently, is to see current ecclesial structures as sinful, not least because the leaders of our church, while they are willing to recognize and try to atone for the sins we Catholics have committed, find themselves unable to admit that the church itself can be sinful. Leave that issue to the theologians for now. But let us be clear that whatever impedes our full humanity is sinful because it impedes the will of God. Structures that settle for or that impose a lesser humanity are sinful. Apartheid was sinful; slavery was sinful; sexism is sinful; and so on. What is harder for people to grasp is that, admittedly on a less drastic level, clericalism is sinful too. It divides the church into two classes of people, where one has voice in the church and one does not. The sinfulness is not that some are ordained and some are not. Any future vision of the church will include such recognition of different charisms. The sinfulness is that the ordained have voice and the non-ordained do not and, perhaps, that admission to the ranks of the ordained usually requires celibacy and always requires maleness. We may never vote for bishops in the Catholic Church, and perhaps we never should. But until the whole people truly has voice, we are all of us—laity and clergy alike—trapped in the sinful structures of clericalist oppression.

Why Should Laypeople Take Responsibility?

There are at least four good reasons why laypeople should take responsibility in the church. In the first place, we are adults and adults take responsibility. Second, it is clear that lately in the American Catholic Church our leaders in the faith have not been doing a very good job, and someone has to fill the credibility gap that their failures have created. Third, we are baptized Christians and baptism into the community obliges us to take responsibility for its integrity. And finally, because the roles that ordained leaders play in the church do not make sense except as symbols of responsibilities that we all possess, their leadership points to our responsibilities.

1. Adults Take Responsibility

When we claim that the lay/clerical relationship needs to move from one of child/parent to one of equality, we are saying that adult behavior among the laity is non-negotiable for laypeople themselves, and that acceptance of the laity as adults is non-negotiable for bishops. For most of the history of the U.S. church, the clergy/laity relationship has been one of parent and child. To a surprising degree this remains true today, especially in New England, easily the most conservative sector of American Catholicism. Often enough, clergy view laity as talented adolescents, people with skills that they themselves may not possess, but not people called to leadership in the church. On the one hand, not infrequently, bishops treat theologians as if they are automatically suspect, instead of being alert to the possibility that they may know more than the bishop does. On the other hand, centuries of infantilization have taken their toll on lay consciousness, and the laity are likely enough to acquiesce to treating the clergy as a child might treat parents. But in fact the whole church desperately needs the adulthood of the laity. The clergy need to let it happen, and the laity need to claim it. The clergy need to see the laity as their equals, not just before God but in the daily life of the church. And the laity need to abandon their fear of speaking out. They need to grow up.

Just as adolescents make the real move into adulthood when they realize that being adult is less about driving cars or having sex than it is about balancing your checkbook and meeting all your responsibilities head-on, so laypeople in the church will achieve adulthood when they see that the accountability they practice in their daily lives needs to be extended to the life of the church. Laypeople have to call the church to accountability, but they also have to be accountable themselves. And that means speaking out, doing the hard work of making oneself and others uncomfortable in the local community of faith until what needs to be done is in fact in process. When everything else has been talked out, the real work of church reform takes place in the local parish, and that can be uncomfortable, whether it means confronting the pastor or one's fellow parishioners.

2. The Laity Need to Fill a Responsibility Gap

One of the remarkable features of the public response to the scandal of sex abuse was the way in which criticism of the bishops was spread across the political spectrum of Catholicism. Admittedly, the likes of Gary Wills and George Weigel, James Carroll, and Richard John Neuhaus found different underlying pathologies and proposed dramatically varied solutions, but they were unanimous in declaring the U.S. bishops, as a whole, to have been remarkably incapable of foreseeing the scandal, culpably ignorant of how seriously the church as a whole would take it, and extraordinarily defensive in dealing with it. For the most part, leadership was missing. Far too many of our bishops, it seemed, were only too ready to emulate the apostles by scurrying into hiding and practicing denial. Who, exactly, among our bishops, stepped forward and grasped the helm of the national church? No one, though we should give Bishop Wilton Gregory some credit for trying.

It seems that we may have some important lessons to learn from the church's distant past about the role of the laity in a crisis. Over sixteen hundred years ago the church was in the grip of the Arian heresy, and its future was by no means secure. Bishops were as likely as anyone else to espouse the views of Arius; and if the church had been forced to follow their lead, today's orthodoxy might look very different from the one we possess. As Cardinal Newman so famously noted, the faith of the church was maintained for the best part of a century by the laity, not by the bishops and presbyters. It is of course not true that our bishops have fallen away from the faith of the church, but nevertheless the example set by the laity in the fourth century is one that could benefit us, namely, that it is the right and responsibility of laypeople to speak out when necessary for the good of the church. This last phrase, by the way, recalls not so much the distant past but rather the words of the bishops at Vatican II a mere forty years ago.

The laity of the early church probably had a less difficult time mobilizing themselves in defense of the faith because they were used to having a significant voice in church governance. Many early church texts provide clear evidence that laypeople were consulted as a matter of course about the work of the church, and especially about the selection of their leaders. Where they did not directly elect them, they were closely involved in the process, perhaps choosing by acclamation from a short list brought before them by the bishops of the province. So, for example, the third-century bishop Cyprian of Carthage was quite clear in his letter to the church that "it is our custom when we make appointments to clerical office to consult you beforehand, and in council with you to weigh the character and qualities of each candidate." Indeed, he is adamant that he has always been committed "right from the beginning of my episcopate, to do nothing on my own private judgment without your counsel and the consent of the people." In *The Apostolic Tradition*, the third-century Roman writer Hippolytus was quite clear that the bishop should be chosen first by all the people (*pantos tou laou*) and subsequently approved by the bishops and presbyters. Origen wrote that "the presence of the laity was essential in Episcopal elections." Pope Leo the Great in the fifth century famously enunciated the principle, "Let the one who is going to rule over all be elected by all," only confirming the words of his predecessor of the previous century, Celestine I, who declared that "a bishop should not be given to those who are unwilling to receive him. The consent and the wishes of the clergy, the people and the nobility are required."

In the years immediately before Vatican II the great French theologian Yves Congar traced the role of this "principle of consent" in the church, by which decisions of church leaders, whether appointments or doctrines, were brought alive. Perhaps doctrines could be true without the consent of the people, said Congar, but they had no living role in the church. We can think of examples today, the best, perhaps, being the failure of the teaching on birth control. In any case, this principle of consent is effectively reborn in the church in Vatican II's teaching on the role of the *sensus fidelium*, by which God's Spirit guides the church by means of the practice of the whole faithful people. And it was surely this renewal that led Cardinal Leo Suenens, one of the great architects of the council, to declare in his great book *Co-responsibility in the Church* (1968) that while it is true that the church is not a democracy, it is undoubtedly true that the church has monarchic, oligarchic, *and* democratic elements. Perhaps the great Belgian churchman should have reversed the order to reflect the chronology. First, the church was democratic, then it became oligarchic, only to find its way to monarchy. But laypeople today have the example of history and the warrant of Vatican II to take their responsibilities for the good of the church enormously seriously.

3. Baptism Entails Responsibility

Vatican II rediscovered the importance of baptism as more than simply a rite of initiation into the community of faith by overcoming a number of obstacles that history had placed in the way. In the first instance, so long as laypeople were taken to have mostly passive roles in the church, few looked beyond baptism as a sacrament of initiation. But once the church was revisioned as an essentially missionary community, then initiation was also entry into mission. Second, the council had to look past the longstanding Catholic tradition of infant baptism, which whatever its merits tends to obscure the sense that the baptized are called to mission. And third, the reemergence of baptism leads inexorably to the restoration of the priesthood of all the baptized, a notion that was all but eclipsed by the Catholic obsession with the nature, rights, and powers of the ordained ministry. While there may be some challenges in the council's insistence on the difference in kind, not merely in degree, between the two priesthoods, it at least has the merit of actually uttering the phrase "baptismal priesthood" once again in Catholic theology.

The council's teaching on baptism as the basis for all mission and ministry does not eliminate the particularity of ordained priesthood. It clarifies the status of ordination, however, as one kind of ministry alongside others, one that involves the charism of leadership of the local community. And it makes clear that, even if one wishes to insist on the "essential" distinction between the two priesthoods, that of all the baptized and that of the ordained, the ordained priesthood is evidently explicable only in relation to that of the baptized. As Cardinal Newman, writing to his fellow clergy, is reputed to have said, "we would look foolish without the laity." This "relational" understanding of ministry, which we touched on briefly in chapter 2, is a fresh emphasis in theological reflection and promotes the idea that the distinctiveness of ordained ministry lies in the particular quality of the relation of the priest to the rest of the community, not in some inner, magical change in his very being.

The relational approach to understanding ministry stresses that in baptism we are inserted into a missionary community and, at least in principle, called to mission. Our mission grows naturally from our particular talents, and the church can recognize this mission in a variety of ways. Ordination is one of these ways, and, like other ministries less directly connected to leadership, ordination places us in a particular relationship to the community of faith, which we did not have before. In ordination, the priest acquires a new *ordo,* a new set of relationships to the community. It is in this new ecclesial relationship that the "real change" involved in ordination is located. Of course, the implication here is that the usual language of the church in which ordination confers an "ontological" or "substantial" change upon the ordinand is a misleading or at least unhelpful way of describing the real change that occurs in ordination.

The language of ontological change, like the language of transubstantiation, is a time-conditioned effort to express the timeless truth of real change or real presence. We are obliged as Catholics to hold to the doctrine of the real presence of Christ in the Eucharist. We are not obliged to find the language of transubstantiation helpful. Similarly, we believe that ordination makes a real difference to the one who is ordained, but we are not obliged to find the language of ontological change helpful. John Paul II frequently spoke of his belief in the qualitative and not merely quantitative difference between the common priesthood of the baptized and hierarchical priesthood. If he means that this priesthood is something more specific, then the distinction is not problematic. The problem is that the language of a qualitative distinction between the two priesthoods has obscured the fact that Christian theology sees the biggest qualitative change occurring at baptism. It is there that we become a new creation. Or to put it another way, to talk of an ontological change occurring at ordination obscures the fact that the real ontological change occurs at baptism.

To say that "real change" occurs in ordination is not to say that "real change" that is equally significant does not occur in the commissioning to ministry of those who are called to other roles in the church. In each case, in precisely similar fashion, the commissioning/ordination places the individual in a new relation to the whole community of faith. In one case, it may be the responsibility of presidency at the Eucharist or leadership of the local church. In another it might be taking charge of catechetics for the parish. Baptized adult members of the faith community are called to place their talents at the service of the whole. These talents must be in evidence before the call comes (seminary directors please note!), and the call must come both from the local community (parish) and the local church (bishop).

From a traditional Catholic point of view, the drawback to this approach to ministry is that it seems to set aside the standard view that the hierarchical ministry of the church is directly established by Christ, not a structure set up by the community itself. However, this does not seem necessarily to follow. In the first place, the very different ministerial structure of the early church was presumably at least as much a reflection of the will of Christ as has been the later development of the divide between clergy and lay. But more important, the focus on the christological origins of priesthood can serve to obscure the pneumatological basis for ministry as a whole. All genuine calling to ministry in the church is the work of the Spirit, expressed in the will of the local church and the local community and finding resonance in the generosity of the individual heart. If it is true that priesthood is structurally different from lay ministry because of its historical origins in a direct act of Christ (which, of course, is often understood far too unhistorically as Jesus' institution of the tripartite ministry of bishop, priest, and deacon), this does not imply that the Spirit acts differently in calling one to leadership and another to teaching. There are many gifts, but one Spirit.

There are many ways in which we might think about the usefulness of the baptismal paradigm. In the first instance it seems to promote a solidarity and equality among Christians that does not obscure but even makes clearer the differences among specific callings. Second, it asks us to think again about the balance between christology and pneumatology in discussions, say, of apostolicity. Yves Congar, for example, believed that the way in which conditions in Nazi-occupied Europe meant that lay Catholics were often asked to do the work usually done by priests was providential. The work of laypeople was not simply a response to a shortage of clergy. The nature of the modern world, he comments presciently, is that, more and more, pastoral necessity will make us see that "the work of the gospel be considered as belonging not to the clergy alone but to the clergy and the laity together." The crucial point is not that our times are short of priests and so the laity can and must take up the slack, but because there is a shortage of priests in our time, it becomes progressively clearer that apostolic activity in its fullness requires the involvement of the laity. The relative profusion of priests in the past has served to hide the apostolicity of the laity. Third, the baptismal paradigm raises important questions about the relative roles of community and bishop in calling people to ministry. Fourth, the idea of vocation as entry into a new ecclesial relationship asks us to think again about the wisdom of the ancient church's insistence that ordination was ordination to service of a particular community. The idea of ordination as we know it today, "absolute" ordination followed by assignment to a particular post, was abhorrent for many centuries. Finally, this relational approach offers the possibility of thinking of all ministry, including that of the ordained, as lasting only as long as the relationship to the community perdures.

4. Ordained Leadership Points to Lay Leadership

The ordained are sacramental symbols of realities possessed by all the faithful in virtue of their baptism into a priestly, missioned people. Bishops, priests, and deacons each have particular responsibilities in the church. Bishops have "oversight," or care for, and leadership of the local church. Priests preserve and uphold church teaching in word and worship. Deacons serve the needs of the local community. In their respective roles ordained ministers are sacraments of a concrete reality that the whole faithful people expresses in virtue of baptism. As Michael Himes has written, if there is a common priesthood, then there is also a common episcopacy and a common diaconate. We are all called to care for the church, to teach and proclaim the word of God, and to serve one another. But our ordained ministers sacramentally symbolize this reality for us, reminding us of what is our common responsibility by virtue of baptism. It is, if you like, a theological parallel to the much older argument that the life of religious vowed to poverty, chastity, and obedience sacramentally symbolizes virtues and values to which the whole community is called. And all of this ties the ministry of the ordained to the baptismal call of all the faithful. The questions we may want to ask about it will center on whether in so doing it obscures the "qualitative difference" between the two kinds of priesthood and, perhaps, whether it matters if it does. But the inestimable advantage of relating the meaning of ordination directly to the concrete reality of the baptized Christian life makes this a risk worth taking.

Bibliographical Note

For a discussion of how the laity were involved in the selection of bishops for many centuries, there are useful essays by Francis A. Sullivan and Michael J. Buckley in an important collection edited by Stephen J. Pope and entitled *Common Calling: The Laity and Governance of the Catholic Church* (Washington, D.C.: Georgetown University Press, 2004). This book and a similar collection edited by Francis Oakley and Bruce Russett, *Governance, Accountability and the Future of the Catholic Church* (New York: Continuum, 2004), taken together are a wonderful resource for the history of the laity in the church and would make excellent reading for parish groups. Cardinal Newman's discussion of the role of the laity in saving the church from Arianism is contained in his famous essay *On Consulting the Faithful in Matters of Doctrine* (New York: Sheed & Ward, 1961). The discussion of relational and ontological change in concepts of ordained ministry is central to Edward Hahnenberg's book *Ministry: A Relational Approach* (New York: Crossroad, 2003) and can be found in shorter form in Richard Gaillardetz's essay "The Ecclesial Foundations of Ministry Within an Ordered Communion," in the collection edited by Susan K. Wood, *Ordering the Baptismal Priesthood: Theologies of Lay and Ordained Ministry* (Collegeville, Minn.: Liturgical Press, 2003). Finally, Michael Himes's suggestion that ordained leadership symbolizes responsibilities that we all possess is contained in an essay entitled "Lay Ministers and Ordained Ministers" in *Lay Ministry in the Catholic Church: Visioning Church Ministry through the Wisdom of the Past*, edited by Richard W. Miller (Liguori, Mo.: Liguori, 2005).

Discussion Questions

1. What can be done in today's church to make normal adult accountability available to the ordained clergy? What is it about the structures of clerical culture that seems to militate against being accountable? Or is this a false problem?
2. What can be done in today's church to get the laity to see that the accountability they practice on a daily basis in their family and professional lives needs also to be employed in the faith community?
3. What structures do we need in today's church to make it possible for the laity to exercise the "principle of consent" discussed by Yves Congar?
4. If baptism is so central to mission and ministry, what can we do to stress this truth in a church committed to infant baptism? Should we move to adult baptism, or should we find a way to give more prominence to the sacrament of confirmation, or what?

Chapter Five

UNDERSTANDING THE
SEX-ABUSE SCANDAL

The Scandal of Sexual Abuse

No one would argue with the statement that at the heart of the sex-abuse scandal that has been plaguing the church for the past few years stands a sizeable number of victims of abuse. Just how many there are, no one will ever know. Those who came forward may be most of the victims, but they cannot be all. Moreover, just as a large number of the abusers are deceased, so there must have been many victims who died unknown, and a church which takes seriously the communion of saints and the resurrection of the body must be ready to recognize that solidarity with victims extends especially to those who died unrequited. And if the effort to understand the scandal of sexual abuse leads us away from a focus on the victims, as it will, we have to return in the end to one question: have we made it at least a little less likely that people will be abused, victimized, and suffer injustice at the hands of the church?

The response to victims and abusers alike must be marked by justice, mercy, and sound pastoral practice. Obviously this means somewhat different things for the two groups. The church has made some progress in the last few years in bringing justice and mercy to the victims, though it is saddening to see that the greatest progress seems to have been made under the threat of litigation. Justice for the victims requires appropriate redress of their grievances, whether that means financial compensation or the provision of therapy or the prosecution of their abusers, or all of the above. Mercy for victims translates into compassionate reception of their complaints. And sound pastoral practice goes beyond this to an effort to draw them back into the community of faith from which they may have become alienated through no fault of their own. This last is the most difficult, perhaps the most important, and has thus far been least attended to.

When we turn to the abusers, we can readily see that justice is most directly going to mean bringing them to account for their crimes. Justice, however, does not stop there. Justice for abusers needs to go on to ask to what degree their criminal behavior was facilitated by the church itself. A dysfunctional family can all too readily be in denial about the failings of its members, and moving abusers from parish to parish or diocese to diocese is as plain a case of enabling as I can imagine. Then justice may also lead to mercy, and we face the need for rehabilitation of the abusers. Obviously, this is a sensitive point. "Rehabilitation" of a kind has been one of the most scandalous failings uncovered in the last couple of years, as abusers have been pronounced cured and released once again on unsuspecting children. But it is not crystal clear that the mercy and compassion that must accompany the necessary and rigorous insistence on justice are visible in the simplistic expediency of the so-called zero-tolerance policy, any more than it is certain that the abusers are the only church personnel who deserve to stand in the dock.

A scandal of such proportions involves many more than the victims and the abusers. Suppose we ask who was responsible. At the center, of course, are the abusers. But in their different ways other groups must take a share of the blame; first, the American bishops, followed by the Vatican, then the parochial clergy, and after them the laity. Perhaps the conservatives are right, too, that American culture itself must take a share of the blame for the extent of sexual abuse of children. Not a few commentators driven by a determination to continue to protect the institution have tried to place a measure of blame on the victims themselves. After all, weren't at least some of them responsible to some degree, and hasn't their litigiousness been a major contributor to the crisis, fanned of course by the greed of lawyers and the grubby exaggerations of the press? And more than one individual has tried to lay the blame on parents for putting their children in harm's way! Such diversionary tactics are rightly considered repulsive by most people. The victims are not responsible, and the words of Jesus insist that "whoever causes one of these little ones who believe in me to stumble, it would be better for him that a huge millstone should be hung around his neck, and that he should be sunk in the depths of the sea" (Matthew 18:6).

When we ask who is hurt most by the scandal, the picture is not quite the same. The group most hurt—after the victims of course— would be those parochial clergy who were not only innocent of abuse but also unaware of it among their fellow clergy. The laity who were unaware would follow closely on them. Next, if hurt means "caused to suffer" rather than simply "damaged," would have to come American society, which surely needs the perspective and priorities that a vigorous Catholicism can bring to the public forum. If we stress the element of damage, however, particularly damage to their credibility, then perhaps next would come bishops and the Vatican, both of whom seem to have isolated themselves fairly successfully from serious psychological trauma, if not systemic harm.

A further question we might ask is, Who has benefited from the fact that the extent of sexual abuse has now become a matter of public awareness? Then we have to draw a very different kind of picture. Most people would put the lawyers and the press at the center here, though it might be better to put the victims first, since the crisis is fundamentally about redressing rather than creating their problems. After that, who benefits most depends on how we see the crisis having salutary effects. Perhaps it might be the bishops, whom public scrutiny has forced into action. But a better answer might be the church as a whole and particularly the laity. Large sections of the laity have been scandalized and energized, and a more adult laity can only be to the benefit of the church. Or can it? Obviously, the question of who benefits can only be answered relative to a vision of the good. In this case, the good of the church. How do we envisage the good of the church? There is no consensus on this. Ecclesiologies are deeply and increasingly reflective of positions drawn on the ideological battlelines of the liberals and the (neo) conservatives. To the latter, the liberals are using the crisis to benefit a vision of the church as just another liberal Protestant denomination, a kind of "Catholic Lite," to use George Weigel's phrase. To the liberals, more conservative types see the crisis as a chance to reassert a preconciliar vision of the church. Both the liberals and the conservatives, of course, would counter these arguments in a similar way. Both would claim to be in defense of a legitimate understanding of Vatican II's ecclesiology.

It is clear, then, that if we stay with the story of the scandal as it has unfolded, without going into questions of meaning, there are too many ends of the stick to get hold of. We can read the crisis in many different ways, and most of them—liberal or conservative—will tend to confirm our own vision of what the church should be and where it ought to be going if it would only listen to us. Worst of all, and perhaps this is the greatest danger at the present time, we can look at the crisis divorced from issues of deeper meaning, perhaps hypnotized by the evil at its heart, and understand it bureaucratically. Then we draw up report cards for the bishops and check on how they are doing at meeting the standards they wrote for themselves. But if there is one thing we can be clear about, it is that what therapists call "the presenting problem" is not in the end successfully addressed unless it is placed in the larger context of systemic issues. Get to the systemic issues and the presenting problem will be dealt with. Don't get to the systemic issues and even if the presenting problem goes away, some other will appear to take its place. In other words, for all its horror, the scandal of sexual abuse is also a symptom of a deeper malaise in the church.

The Underlying Problem

Let us be clear. Sex abuse in the church is a scandal, but it is not a crisis. There is no sex-abuse crisis in the church. What the church suffers from is a crisis issuing from the real problem of clerical sexual abuse of minors. Sex abuse itself is a heinous crime and a scandal in the church of the highest magnitude. But it isn't in itself a crisis. First, the numbers of abusers are not inordinately large, as far as we can tell, and the statistical evidence puts the rate of abuse among clergy significantly below the rate of abuse by adult males as a whole. Of course, there are two corollaries that give cause for concern. One is that clergy are expected to stand in a particular relationship of trust toward laity and most especially toward children (though one cannot resist saying that parents—who statistically do most of the abusing—are also trampling on an equally solemn trust). And the other is that by far the majority of the victims have been post-pubescent males, whereas in the population at large adolescent girls and young women are the preferred targets of the mostly male predators. Second, while one has to treat the statistics carefully, it seems as if the incidence of abuse has declined over the past ten to twenty years. Whether this is because traumatized victims have not (yet) come forward, or because there are simply fewer priests out there than there used to be, or because they are older, or because seminary training is better than it was, it is hard to say. Third, however late in the day, the bishops do seem to have made some efforts to address the scandal, and to have had some success in dealing fairly with victims and perpetrators. There is even, apparently, some restoration of confidence among sectors of the laity, though for the first time in our history the percentage of Catholics at weekly worship is lower than that of their Protestant counterparts.

It is a much more accurate statement of the present reality, then, to say that the scandal of clerical sexual abuse of minors has thrown the church into crisis. It is also important to insist on describing the problem this way, and instructive to see that the Vatican and the bishops have a distinct preference for clinging to the language of the crisis of sexual abuse. The good work that the American bishops and their watchdog commissions (staffed mostly by laypeople) have done to address sex abuse will hopefully mean that this problem in its current dimensions will never trouble the church again. That would certainly be the hope of all of us. But if we call this "the crisis" and are able to declare it "solved" or at least taken seriously, then human nature being what it is, there will be an inclination on the part of church leaders to return to business as before. If it is true, however, that the particular scandal has revealed deeper structural problems, then the successful overcoming of the scandal is not at all the same thing as dealing with the crisis. Only if we can deal with the real crisis can we have any confidence that such scandals might be less likely to happen in the future.

The scandal of sexual abuse revealed a crisis of episcopal leadership. Poor leadership in dealing with the scandal has led to the kind of public scrutiny to which bishops are not accustomed. The precise nature of the crisis is not something that all will agree upon, but its elements are evident. To name them is not to accuse every American bishop of all the elements, but to point to systemic problems to which all American bishops must attend. Among the charges that have been made over the past few years are the following: a faulty understanding of what it is to be a leader on the part of those who select bishops, and a consequent lack of good leaders within the episcopacy; bad judgment about how the good name of the church can best be assured; secrecy; isolation; ambition and careerism; poor theology; too centralized an understanding of the church, with a concomitant overdeference to the Roman Curia; excessive bureaucratization of the role of the bishop. Some or all of these may be accurate, but not all qualify as systemic issues. Inappropriate ambition, for example, is something that systemic problems can foster, but in itself it is a personal rather than a structural sin.

Beyond the crisis in the episcopate there is a deeper ecclesiological crisis that is at the same time a cultural crisis. Church historians know that structures of government in the church have changed over time and have indeed always been changing, but, what is more important, that these changes have paralleled changes in secular understandings of government. They have usually needed to stress this in the teeth of those who see the first and last word on ecclesiology to be that "the church is not a democracy." At a major conference just a few years ago, the opening keynote address was given by a distinguished bishop who tried to make the case that Jesus pretty much envisaged the church as it exists today. Either the bishop believed this, which is sheer historical ignorance, or he thought we needed to hear this, which is insulting. And in an action that revealed so much, he then promptly left the meeting and did not hear the impressive array of distinguished Catholic historians, who deal in historical fact, and, entirely unintentionally, made his presentation seem bogus and frankly ridiculous. If only he had stayed to hear Francine Cardman challenge the proponents of what she called "default ecclesiology" to recognize that the church is not monolithic but "a dynamic, evolving, diverse movement," or Brian Tierney explain that "within the Catholic church there have always been these three, Peter, the apostles, and the people of God, but the constitutional relationships between them have been defined differently in different ages," or Marcia Colish point out that while secular governments have continued to change throughout history, becoming constitutional monarchies and then representative democracies with no kings or queens, "the church remained trapped in the absolute monarchy time warp of the early modern period," or Frank Oakley offering up the conciliarist movement as a phenomenon that has much still to teach us, though it has been consigned to the garbage heap of church history by what Oakley calls "an ultramontane politics of oblivion," or John Beal's eloquent call for a canon law that restores the balance between *communio* and juridic ecclesiologies. Now is surely the time to answer the question with which Oakley ended his paper: "with what confidence, after all, can we Catholics hope to erect a future capable of enduring if, for ideological reasons, we persist in trying to do so on the foundation of a past that never truly was?"

The weight of the historical evidence would strongly suggest that it is quite appropriate to ask how democratic sensibilities might have something important to offer to the church today, and that it is entirely probable that the church will evolve, willy-nilly, to incorporate some genuine role for the voice of the whole community into its structures of governance. It has been so in the church's past, most recently in the American church of the eighteenth and early nineteenth centuries, and it could be so again. The lessons of history also teach us, however, that it is exceedingly rare that an elite in any society will freely give up its own hold on power. And this brings us to what may be a yet deeper level of the crisis, namely, an ecclesiology and a polity that gives no formal role to the voice of laypeople in the church to which they belong, buttressed by the sorry history of theological reflection upon the laity. Here is where the discussion of clericalism belongs. Clericalism can be damaging and can be petty. It can be ridiculous and it can be scandalous. It can be as sinister as it is in John Gregory Dunne's *True Confessions* and as comic as it is in J. F. Powers's incomparable stories of the lives of clergy. But in the end it always points to the real issue that for at least three quarters of the church's life the best theological definition the church could offer of the layperson was "not clergy."

Fear of History

A great theologian once wrote that it takes two constitutive principles to make a living church, the principle of structure and the principle of life. The first of these is the responsibility of the bishops. They are the ones who give the church its structure. But over the course of time there has been an excessive focus on their role, such that the balancing principle of life has been overlooked. This is the work of the whole people, and throughout at least the early history of the church was the particular responsibility of the laity, as they consented to something as big and amorphous as doctrine, or something as local and practical as the selection of a bishop. So a healthy church needs to recover the balance of the hierarchical constitution of the church with the cooperation of the faithful, through which life is breathed into the otherwise true but sterile structure. It is sad that the church has tended to overstress the communion of the parts *with* the hierarchy as the principle of structure, instead of the communion *between* the parts, namely, between the hierarchical ministry and the community of the faithful within which all, clergy and laity together, exist. Catholic unity resides above all in the will of the parts to behave as members of one body, regulated by the power of the Holy Spirit. Because this emphasis has been played down in the post-Reformation church, the faithful are unaware of their responsibility to make the church. The passivity of the laity, in other words, often passed off as the historical accident of an unlettered people, is a result of conscious choices on the part of the leadership. The principle of structure, it would seem, does not easily warm to the Spirit that blows where it will.

The suggestion that the two principles of structure and life have been unequally treated in the past several hundred years brings us back once again to accountability. The higher sense of accountability as a "deeper mutuality," which we identified in chapter 3, corresponds very closely to the idea that there should be a communion *between* the parts of the church and not merely a communion *of* the parts *with* the hierarchy. It is, in the end, the role of the bishops to teach, and it is the function of the whole people, mostly laity, to breathe life into this teaching (or not) as the Spirit moves them. But both sets of duties only make sense when they are in the service of the covenantal relationship that binds the church together and that binds it to God. The Spirit is at work everywhere in the church, of course, but when we encounter disagreement or apparent conflict between the role of the bishops and the life of the community of faith, it is helpful to remember that the Spirit cannot be at war with itself. When there are disputes or differences of opinion within the church, the Holy Spirit is at work in that dispute, and both "sides" cannot be equally correct. Long term, the principle of life seems to have the edge over particular decisions of particular church leaders at particular moments in history. Short term, however, the principle of life can be too easily invoked to reject a teaching that the faithful find difficult. This, for example, is why it seems clear that the papal teaching on birth control has not been wise or helpful, on the one hand, and why, on the other, American Catholic disinclination to accept the episcopal teaching that capital punishment is always wrong should not be canonized as the voice of the Spirit.

We can enlarge our consideration of the roots of our church's crisis by paying attention to the parallels between the ways in which secular society and the church have developed in the modern world. One helpful approach begins by recognizing that any integrated and successful society is marked by cooperation and a common purpose between the human or community dimension and the systems that need to be used to manage the whole panoply of its non-human interactions (science, technology, the everyday manipulation of the environment). But in the modern world it is too often true that the system shakes off the authority of the human community that gave birth to it and, driven by imperatives of money, markets, and power, comes to have autonomous existence, even impinging on the specifically human and driving human interaction into purely private realms. That which was an expression of the community has now made the community an expression of itself. The two spheres belong in an equilibrium in which the system is seen to serve the lifeworld. John Paul II came very close to this vision when in his encyclical *Laborem Exercens* (On Human Work, 1982) he referred critically to "the instrumentalization of labor to capital," insisting that a healthy society should show the reverse, the instrumentalization of capital to labor, of "stuff" to people. It is, of course, in a parade of irony that we see so often in the life of the church that it is one thing to promote a democratic social order and quite another to extend it to the workings of the church.

It is an easy transposition to put this overall theory to work in the context of the church. The church is a community of faithful people, equal by virtue of their baptism, celebrating the freedom of the children of God promised in the gospel. But like any human community that will perdure in time, it has a public, institutional face. The institutional superstructure or system exists to aid the functioning of the community as what it is, in this case, a community of faith that believes in Jesus Christ. The institutional element with its institutional methods exists to serve the community of faith. But this institutional element, at least in the Catholic tradition, has a history of overstepping its bounds, identifying the church with its own imperatives, forgetting that it exists to serve. When that happens, the open communication that should mark human interactions is replaced by more manipulative practices. Among them is a shift from a leadership based on moral authority to one based on power, or more likely the confusion of the two. This, for example, could help explain the often-noted ambiguity of our collective response to John Paul II. He had enormous personal attributes that inspired great respect and caused him in many ways to be an extraordinary leader. At the same time, he often seemed to lead in an authoritarian fashion. The more critical judgments made of his pontificate as a whole are rarely if ever challenging his legitimate gifts, but rather pointing to the ways in which—to return to language we used in chapter 2— the structural oppression at work in the church oppressed even him.

If we draw such a parallel between church and society in modernity, we should not assume that the changes in the institutional church during these last two hundred years always occurred by accident. There are those who believe that the form of the church that prevailed in the century and a half before Vatican II was developed in conscious reaction to the Enlightenment and out of fear of modernity. It may be that the church very consciously drew on elements of modernity itself in order to create a church that could stand against the modern world. In other words, in order to protect a premodern view of the church against the normal processes of historical development to which the church, like other historical bodies, is subject, the institution adopted the mechanisms of modernity.

If this is true, we come up with a persuasive explanation for the growth of a centralized bureaucratic Catholicism. It additionally strengthens the story, told so well by the great historian of American Catholicism Jay Dolan, of how the remarkably liberal American Catholicism of the late eighteenth century was transformed into the ultramontane empire of the nineteenth. As Dolan charts the story, when the papacy begins to revive in the first quarter of the nineteenth century it increasingly insists on dismantling the American system in favor of a Roman model. But why it does this, and especially why it can enlist the help of so many American churchmen in the execution of its policies, is not satisfactorily explained solely in terms of European lack of sympathy for American culture.

The theory that the church adopted elements of modernity in order to fight modernity itself also helps to explain what happened at Vatican II, and perhaps the reactions to it during subsequent papacies. The majority of the bishops at Vatican II consciously battled a vision of the church maintained by the ecclesiastical bureaucracy and, in most estimations, defeated it soundly during the first session of the council. The challenge was to the modern centralized and bureaucratized Catholicism that had emerged in the course of the nineteenth century and become entrenched during the reigns of the three Piuses. Its features included suspicion of intellectual modernity, controls over the community through the promotion of forms of devotion and worship that had their origins in baroque European piety, and centralized control of the universal church. But the council produced a much more positive evaluation of modernity; it sought to reform Catholic worship, devotion, and practice, and it encouraged distinctive expressions of Catholicism appropriate to the different cultures in which it had taken root around the world. While Paul VI somewhat nervously promoted this cultural differentiation, John Paul II's reign was marked by efforts to undo it. His writings grew more and more suspicious of contemporary culture, and in particular of the so-called hedonism and ethical relativism of American society. He advocated traditional forms of piety, especially Marian piety and Eucharistic adoration, in ways that we have not seen since Pius X, and showed considerable suspicion of liturgical variations that reflected local cultures. Above all, he sought to recentralize the church by, among other things, promoting the quasi infallibility of the ordinary magisterium and undermining the authority of national bishops' conferences.

In conclusion, we need to return to John Beal's call for balance and Cardinal Bernardin's hope for common ground. The problem is not that the institution is bad and the community of faith is good. The community of faith will always have an institutional face. The problem is that too much power has shifted to the institution, and the church is in consequence off center. That this has happened because of the church's suspicion of modernity seems very likely. The result of the imbalance is certainly bad. The historical chickens have come home to roost, and in the end it is not surprising that the center of the crisis is the American church. On the one hand, it remains the most vibrant of churches in the so-called developed world. On the other, its increasingly vocal and well-educated laity, roused to action by the scandal of sexual abuse, represents a movement for potential reform that cannot be controlled in the ways the clergy can, and that is feeding off two centuries of the American experiment in democracy. An open society is always better than a closed society. This is the unshakeable conviction of thinking people in a society that strives to be democratic. The crisis in the church will not go away until we find ways to make the church into the open society that, at the present time, it is certainly not.

In sum, the history of the church has shown a tension between the institutional and the charismatic, juridical, and *communio* ecclesiologies—the principle of structure and the principle of life, christology and pneumatology. This is unproblematic until serious imbalances arise, and when they do we have an ecclesiological crisis on our hands. The latest crisis has been brewing for two hundred years, as the church bureaucratized and centralized itself in a defensive reaction to modernity. Oblivious to the role of the Spirit and the principle of life and in the name of defending faith, the institution has defended only itself. It has created a professional class, self-perpetuating and self-policing, insulated from the people by lifestyle and the possession of all executive and legislative authority. The evils of sexual abuse are a direct but epiphenomenal consequence of this bureaucratic blindness. But cultural forces cannot be indefinitely withstood, particularly if they are of the Spirit. The increasingly loud voice of faithful, well-educated lay Catholics demanding a role in the church that, even when they are unaware of it, has a long historical pedigree and considerable theological justification would seem to be just such a Spirit-inspired initiative.

Bibliographical Note

The remarks by Francine Cardman, John Beal, Frank Oakley, Marcia Colish, and Brian Tierney can be found in the collection mentioned at the end of the previous chapter, *Governance, Accountability and the Future of the Catholic Church.* There are many books on the history and significance of the sex-abuse scandal, among them are *Sex, Priests, and Secret Codes: The Catholic Church's 2,000-Year Paper Trail of Sexual Abuse,* by Thomas P. Doyle, A. W. R. Sipe, and Patrick

J. Wall (Los Angeles: Volt Press, 2006), and *Keep the Faith, Change the Church: The Battle by Catholics for the Soul of Their Church*, by James Muller and Charles Kenney (Rodale Books, 2004). A useful discussion of the relationship between Jesus and the early church occupies chapter 2 of Bernard Prusak's *The Church Unfinished: Ecclesiology Through the Centuries* (Mahwah, N.J.: Paulist Press, 2004). The reference to Jay Dolan is to his most recent and most accessible book, *In Search of an American Catholicism* (New York: Oxford, 2003), a book that works very well with parish groups. If you want to pursue the more academic question of the church's relationship to modernity, then the best book is *Catholicism and Liberalism*, edited by R. Bruce Douglass and David Hollenbach (New York: Cambridge University Press, 1994), especially the essay by Joseph Komonchak, "Vatican II and the Encounter Between Catholicism and Liberalism," pp. 76–99. The best Web resources are to be found at Boston College's Twenty-First Century Initiative (http://www.bc.edu/church21/), the National Catholic Reporter (http://www.ncrnews.org/abuse/), and http://www.bishopaccountability.org/.

Discussion Questions

1. How do you understand the relationship between Jesus and the church? Have you ever been aided by the church in taking history and theology seriously?
2. What kinds of practices or structures need to be changed to make communion more a matter of communion *between* hierarchy and laity, and less one of communion of the laity *with* the hierarchy?
3. The church is a great champion of human freedom in the secular world. What can we learn from this about the place of freedom within the church?
4. Consider the connotations of the following four words and the role they play in the local and the national church today: authority, power, leadership, empowerment.

Chapter Six

AN OPEN CHURCH IN
AN OPEN SOCIETY

There have been a lot of words in this book about the notion of an open church in an open society, and it is time to draw some hard conclusions about the characteristics of such a church, and about how these might lead to a future church with a different approach to ministry, to voice, and to accountability.

Characteristics of an Adult Church

1. Knowledge Not Ignorance

Let us begin with the *Da Vinci Code*, a controversy now happily faded into the middle distance, perhaps because of the poor quality of the movie, which hoped to deliver to an even larger audience the sorry mess of intellectual nonsense the book had represented for the many millions who read it. What was really striking about the response of Catholics to the phenomenon was the clear sense that church leaders saw the book as a threat to faith, and indeed that many who read the book seemed quite prepared to accept that its story of Jesus, Mary Magdalene, and the blood line of their descendants was thoroughly plausible. There were far too few Catholics like the woman from Darien, Connecticut, who wrote to her diocesan paper to cancel her subscription, telling them that it was ridiculous to advise readers that it was a sin to read the book or see the movie, still worse to instruct them in appropriate acts of penance for wasting their time and money in such a way.

The sadness of the institutional response to the *Da Vinci Code* is that it could be a threat only to those who are woefully ignorant of the early history of the church, and be perceived to be an occasion of sin or to imperil faith only by leaders who were unable to trust the knowledge and judgment of the great mass of the faithful. The fact that the overwhelming majority of American Catholics possess the intellectual capacity to learn something about church history but know absolutely nothing about it is a scandal. Ignorance of history is a scandal (literally, a stumbling block) to a truly living faith, and until recently the entire responsibility for this sorry situation has lain with the clerical leadership of the church. As adults, laypeople have the responsibility to learn something about history, and as educated people a large number of them are perfectly capable of doing this for themselves. As we noted earlier, however, history is liberating. Those who arm themselves with even a little historical knowledge should not expect a welcome from an establishment that thrives on an entirely ahistorical understanding of the church. The judgment on those who wish to maintain the stumbling block of historical ignorance ought to be severe.

The acquisition of the knowledge necessary to understand the world and to make informed judgments about it is the responsibility of every adult citizen. This is no less true of the demands that adult members of the church should make upon themselves. We cannot allow structures or sheer laziness, either that of the clerical establishment or our own inertia, to keep us from knowing what we need to know to take appropriate responsibility for our church, and to be able to hear and understand and even judge the quality of what we hear from the pulpit and the arguments the church may make for this or that change, and the injunctions to do this, that, or the other thing. Knowledge is also the precondition for the discernment that equips us to know when it is appropriate to submit to the authority or expertise of our ecclesiastical leaders, and when they are exceeding their authority and we need to stand up to them.

2. Inclusivity, Not Exclusivity

From questions of intercommunion to those about access to the Eucharist for divorced and remarried Catholics, from how gays and lesbians may live responsibly in the church to how married people should express themselves sexually, from who can be ordained to what ex-priests may do in the community of faith, from how we treat our theologians to how we treat our politicians, the church seems so often to be in the business of exclusion. Ecumenical dialogue is almost dead because ecumenists have taken things about as far as they can, and the institution has balked at the concrete steps that must come next. Those in the church who arguably need the help of the sacraments most—the divorced and remarried or gays and lesbians in committed relationships—are all but excluded from reception. The gifts of resigned priests may not be placed at the service of the church. Independent theological voices, especially among the clergy, are commonly disciplined and sometimes lose their jobs. Catholic politicians trying to balance the competing demands of their public trust and their religious identity are pilloried if they seem not to conform to the church's teaching on abortion, though not if they ignore the church's teaching on war. Those who can most help the church move forward pastorally, theologically, spiritually, and even politically are more likely to be objects of suspicion than approval. All in all, the orientation is to exclusion rather than inclusion.

The problem of Catholic exclusivism does not derive from a strong sense of identity but from a weak structure of communication. The tendency toward exclusion is more commonly a sign of insecurity than confidence. We fear what we do not understand, and what we fear we expel, if it is within our power. None of this would have to occur if we were a community in which all sides talked to one another, and in which our appointed leaders were at least as good at listening as they are at pronouncing. The church would obviously be very different if bishops had systematically listened to the voices of women, or to the experience of gays and lesbians, or to the views of the divorced or resigned clergy or working theologians. That they have not done so is very unfortunate. But that we do not have structures within our church that would facilitate these kinds of interactions and more is a scandal of our own making. It is also one that we could relatively easily undo.

Creating the conditions for a more adult church will require us to insist on a thoroughly inclusive attitude. An adult church will be a welcoming church. As a church of sinners, an adult church will particularly welcome other sinners. The church is the community of sinners who are saved through Jesus Christ from the consequences of their sin. The church is not the church when its inclination is to stress its own holiness and impose "correctness" filters—political, lifestyle, or otherwise. Precisely how we are to go about insisting on an inclusive church is not clear, because we are once more faced with the ecclesial Catch-22. How can we remake the church as a more open community when it is not sufficiently open to be able to hear the voices calling for a more open community?

3. Forward Looking, Not Backward Looking

Vatican II represented the definitive opening of the church to the world, symbolized so nicely in Karl Rahner's description of the council as "the coming of the world church." The fundamental conciliar definition of the church as "the people of God" and the vision of cooperation between church and world enshrined in every paragraph of the great concluding document, the Pastoral Constitution on the Church in the Modern World (*Gaudium et Spes*), were intended definitively to put to rest the fearful, isolationist, and self-ghettoized "fortress Catholicism" of the Counter Reformation. But, imperceptibly at first, then more and more boldly, reactionary forces within the church have conspired to return us to these bad old days, most often by employing the myth that liberals somehow kidnapped the council message. Anyone who reads the history of the struggles at the council (history again!) can be in no doubt that this is simply nonsense. The bishops at Vatican II chose a more open understanding of the church over against the defensive, closed vision offered to them by the curial bureaucracy that had drafted the pre-liminary schemas upon which the final documents were expected to be based.

As a clear illustration of this movement, there is no better exam-ple than the current state of our liturgy. The first reforms issuing from the council fathers concerned liturgical change, and these have been the changes that have had the most direct impact on the faith-ful as a whole. Not all the changes were handled sensitively, of course, but on the whole they were successfully completed; and after forty or so years we have largely become accustomed to a more participa-tory Eucharist, in which laypeople have played important roles alongside those of the clergy. Before Vatican II the shape of the liturgy gave the clear impression that the Eucharist was the act of the priest, which laypeople were privileged to witness. Since the council, liturgy clearly communicates the first principle of liturgy, that the Eucharist is the act of the whole community, not that of the priest alone.

Over the last ten years, pressure from some sectors of the Roman Curia, aided by conservative bishops and lay Catholics in North America, has been exerted to reverse some elements of liturgical change. There is, of course, little or no chance that we could ever return to the Tridentine Mass in its full preconciliar mode, but there are subtle forces at work whose efforts will re-insinuate into the liturgy some subliminal and some more overt messages that "restor-ing balance" to the liturgy means taking just a step or two backward. These moves are most apparent in two areas: efforts to reduce the visibility of lay ministers at the Eucharist and adjustments of liturgi-cal language. In the first instance, two documents issued over the past fifteen years have represented the role of eucharistic ministers as effectively a necessary evil, temporary and clearly subordinate aux-iliaries to a priest who alone would take too long to distribute com-munion to a church full of Sunday worshipers. In the second, the longstanding efforts to provide an elegant and recognizable English translation of the liturgy finally succumbed in 2006 to the pressure of a few Vatican officials to return to language "closer to the original Latin"—which is, of course, further from the English language.

If liturgical change is simply where most Catholics see and feel the effects of decisions taken elsewhere, there are many other instances of the efforts to reverse the initiatives of the council. Over the past quarter of a century, national bishops' conferences have been the target of efforts to reduce their authority, moves that limit the real commitment to episcopal collegiality evident at Vatican II. Only two kinds of people are cheered by this step: the Roman Curia, who perceive their power and control to be threatened when initiatives are taken at the national or regional level, and individual bishops of whatever ideological stripe who want to be left alone to run their own dioceses without the intrusion of their brother bishops in national conference. While on the subject of episcopal collegiality, we should also mention the evisceration of the Roman Synod of Bishops, instituted by Vatican II as a practical expression of the responsibility of the worldwide episcopate for leadership of the church. Under John Paul II, following on Paul VI's eventual lack of enthusiasm for a structure he had originally welcomed, the synod had become an exercise in futility, in which the elected bishops were told what to talk about and had no executive role at all.

The ecclesial Catch-22 is particularly apparent when we search around for an answer to a backward-looking church, because our own leaders are either too blind or too fearful to see that it is within their power to act in the pastoral interest of the American church and reject the moves to curtail the legacy of the council. Many, perhaps most, American bishops resent to some degree the intrusion of Rome into issues that are best settled at the national or regional level. A few certainly do not. But how can they express themselves through the bishops' conferences or the Roman Synod when these venues are the sites of the very efforts to quiet them that they ought to be resisting? Not being a bishop, one is tempted to say that they should just say no. It is hard to imagine that if the U.S. bishops presented a united front on, say, the appropriate language for the liturgy, Rome would not cave in. But the bishops would need to be sure that they had the will to resist Rome and, even less likely, that they could summon a united front. Their situation is not exactly like that of the laity, but not in the end totally different. For the laity, there are no approved structures through which they can express themselves; for the episcopacy, there are certainly approved structures, but a word from Rome and they police themselves. It seems as if they have not internalized the words of the council on their collegial responsibilities, or perhaps that they perceive the church in a more secular fashion than is truly the case.

4. Service Oriented, Not Careerist

In an adult church, leadership will be exercised for the good of the local church and never for the personal advancement of the current bishop or pastor. It is sad that the opposite is all too often the case at the present time. In the early church, the idea that a bishop was married to the diocese for which he was chosen was a solemn truth. When, in the ninth century, Bishop Formosus of Porto was elected pope, this was the first time a bishop of Rome had previously been a bishop elsewhere. Indeed, after his death and burial his body was exhumed by his successor and placed on trial and all his decisions were declared invalid because, since he had previously been bishop elsewhere, he could not validly occupy the see of Rome. We certainly do not want to return to the scandalous days of the ninth-century church, but the warning against careerism remains salutary, if extreme. In today's church, every appointment is a stepping stone to higher rank or greater responsibility with a concomitant increase in power and influence. The structure of the diocesan ministry corresponds closely to that of a corporate-career structure, though the oversight against corporate corruption or failure provided in theory by boards of directors is lacking in the case of the church. Of course, to describe the structure in this way is not at all to say that all the clergy or all the bishops collaborate in the career structure. But it does, unfortunately, mean that on the whole it is those who recognize and skillfully manipulate the career structure who rise into its higher ranks. While most bishops may not be ambitious careerists, ambitious careerists in the clerical ranks stand a much higher chance of achieving plum parishes or their own diocese than do those who simply try to serve the community of faith to which they have been called.

While careerism is a huge problem, the solution is relatively simple. It would not be at all difficult for the church to reassert the idea that a bishop is married to his diocese. While this would certainly limit careerism, what would it mean in a situation in which a poor choice had been made. Would a diocese be stuck with such problems for a generation or more? To guard against this possibility, it would be necessary, in the first place, to put far more power into the hands of the local church, with the laity in prominent roles in the selection of their pastors and bishops. Leadership is always exercised locally, and suitable leaders are more likely to be selected when the political or ideological litmus test imposed from above is balanced by a realistic sense of the needs of the local church. Moreover, term limits might be an even better idea in ecclesiastical life than they are in secular politics.

The Local Church of the Future: Adult and Accountable

No one's crystal ball is entirely cloudless, and it would be a foolish person who was too sure of the shape that the church of the future will take. But this chapter, indeed this book, would not be complete without an effort to sketch out some of the features that an adult church will have to exhibit. It remains entirely possible, of course, that the struggle for a more adult church will fail, at least for a time, and that the worst features of the present situation will become even more entrenched, while the congregation dwindles until it is only the passive and obedient few kneeling humbly in the pews of their masters. For now, let us assume that this will not happen, that the church will move forward to express the vision of Vatican II far more effectively than has so far been the case, and that an adult and accountable church that prizes knowledge over ignorance, that is inclusive, forward-looking, and service-oriented will emerge even more clearly. What might it look like?

1. Ministry

While the way we explain ministry may not change much, the outward shape of ministry will be different because the lock on ordained ministry currently held by male celibates will have been broken. This is essential to the future of an adult church, not so much because our ordained ministers are currently celibate as because the concentration of all formal teaching and leadership in the ranks of the celibate clergy impoverishes the church. To enrich our understanding of ministry it is going to be necessary to bring an end to mandatory celibacy. The truth is that large numbers among the present clergy agree that the time for this change has come, and worldwide the practice of celibacy among the diocesan clergy is spotty, to say the least. Equally importantly, as far as we can see, the restriction of ordained ministry to celibate men will continue to mean a decline in the numbers of clergy relative to the numbers of Catholics, and a concomitant loss of access to the Eucharist for laypeople. This of course must force the church to ask itself: which is more important, access to the Eucharist or the maintenance of a celibate clergy, because we cannot have both?

Once mandatory celibacy is a thing of the past, ordained ministers will increasingly be married, with or without children, and will in all probability exercise their ministry in a "parochial team" context that will enable some, if not most, of them to continue to hold weekday jobs. This seems to be the inevitable consequence of a shift to married clergy, at least unless Catholic laypeople are ready to begin financially to support their churches and church personnel on a level more like that of their Protestant and Jewish counterparts. But even if they were, the advantages to the ministry of having people with wider professional experience in their ranks might outweigh the more often suggested value of having a minister at the disposition of the parish 24/7. I am not so sure that someone who is also a plumber or an accountant is necessarily adding to the skills valuable to an ordained minister, though they are probably not detracting from them; but those who are educators or psychologists or physicians might easily enrich their ministry through the additional experience to which they can lay claim.

A second consequence of drawing at least some of the candidates for ordination from among noncelibates is that it will remove the drastic dividing line between what today we call priests and lay ministers. Not much will change theologically, but simple redescription will have an enormous impact. Now we will talk of the responsibility of all the baptized for the church's mission to the world, while recognizing that a minority have a special calling from the Spirit of God, validated in the confirmation of the local community, to serve the community of faith itself. Some of these will be called to a ministry of leadership, including eucharistic presidency, while others will be called to minister to the local community in a variety of different ways. Their respective callings are different from but are built upon their prior baptismal calling to ministry, and all in their different ways are ordered to the call to the whole church to mission to the world.

So important is it to stress the connection between ordination and a calling to lead the local community of faith that it entails consequences for how the title "bishop" needs to be employed in the church. Specifically, there seems to be little warrant for assigning the title to someone who does not have what we used to call "the cure of souls." While there is little reason to deny the title "bishop emeritus" to one who has gone from a diocese to serve in the Roman Curia, there is no justification for using the title of "bishop" to indicate a Roman promotion. It ought to be clear that if you are not a bishop of somewhere, then you are not a bishop. Incidentally, the removal of such honorifics from the job description of Vatican bureaucrats might help ensure that their ranks are more likely to be filled with the few truly called to the rare vocation of administration, and dissuade from struggling to join them those merely looking for advancement.

2. Voice

The single biggest need in the process of creating a more adult church is to allow a genuine voice for the entire body of the faithful. If there are some who have no opportunity to have input in decision making, then they are the ones whom the system infantilizes. The word "voice" is used here, then, in the way you would find it used in an election, where a distinction is often made between "active" and "passive" voice. The former, active voice, is the right to vote, whereas passive voice is the right to stand for election and be elected. In the church, we are not necessarily so concerned with direct elections, though it is probable that there are a number of ecclesial decisions that could be made smoothly in that way. But we are certainly concerned with the more fundamental meaning of the democratic process, namely, the right of all within the community to have a say in the way in which the community is organized.

While laypeople in the Catholic Church have no formal voice in its deliberations, there are a number of venues in which laypeople could be heard. The most obvious examples are parochial and diocesan pastoral and financial councils, diocesan synods when they are called, and diocesan oversight boards set up to monitor compliance with the Charter for the Protection of Young People. Even less formally, laypeople can be heard in newspapers, through organizations of one kind or another, and even in Web logs, or blogs. A healthy church will show evidence of all such kinds of involvement and more. But it will remain an infantilized laity until such time as their voice is used in deliberative contexts, contributing to the formation of teaching, or aiding in the selection of a bishop.

The various changes in ministry that we imagined in the previous section cannot come about without new structures through which the lay voice is channeled for the good of the church. Some of these changes could happen through paternalistic decision making on the part of clerical leadership, but we would still not be living in an adult church. In other words, married clergy or even women clergy would not of themselves represent a new church, whereas structures that endowed the laity with more than the solely advisory role to which all of their activity is currently limited might very well help change the exclusionist mentality of the clerical establishment in more fundamental ways. Voice, not mere change, is the *sine qua non* for ecclesial renewal.

If this is indeed the case, then the face of the future church will include the recognition that all sectors of the church have a legitimate voice in the formation of teaching, the selection and evaluation of leaders, and decisions about the common practices of the church.

To this extent, the church will need to release from within itself its own democratic past and potential. For centuries there was a democratic element at work in the church, but it has long been replaced by more than a thousand years of imperial and despotic political practice, so much so that general approval usually greets any Catholic who pronounces in public, "the church is not a democracy." If this means that elections are not the be-all and end-all of every ecclesial decision, fine. If it means that the church is not structured in such a way that all its members participate in celebrating its present and making its future, then more's the pity.

3. Accountability

The overwhelming experience of people in the lay workday world is that accountability is the order of the day. Accountability is the way in which an open society is true to itself and in which its officials are kept faithful to their responsibilities. The legal system is the fundamental structure of accountability to which all are subject. But there are particular structures of accountability for political leaders, which might include everything from a senator's visit to her state for a town meeting to Congress impeaching a president. The existence of structures signals that the given society expects its members and especially its leaders to live up to their calling. When they fail, they are called to account.

It is sad that the church possesses no structures of accountability for its leaders. Imagine trying to impeach a bishop. All are, of course, subject to church and civil law. But there is no way in which bishops and clergy can be brought before the bar of ecclesial public opinion. No doubt, some at least of their failings can lead to ecclesiastical censure of some kind, but if it happens, it is something conducted completely within the clerical subculture.

One of the more striking acts of exercising voice that one might imagine would be participation in a periodic performance review of the pastor or bishop, conducted by those whom they have been appointed to serve. There is no good reason why the people of the diocese should not periodically evaluate their bishop's performance, or why parishioners should not give feedback to their pastor. And yet the very idea sounds so preposterous, doesn't it? This can only be because these days we almost completely fail to understand the role of the bishop relative to the community of faith.

While we might not want to go back to fourth-century Milan or Hippo and to the way in which the local community in those two cities more or less pressganged Ambrose and Augustine into service as bishop, there are important signals there to realities that we have lost sight of over the centuries. There should be a role for the local community in the selection of the bishop, but currently there is none. The top–down process under which we now suffer, in which bishops are selected in secret by a few clerical power brokers, came into existence originally to protect the church from control by secular authorities. That problem does not exist today in most parts of the world, though we might make an exception for China. In North America, certainly, there are no such worries. A first step in the right direction would be to allow the process that does exist on paper to be activated, so that the local community would be consulted periodically about the list each diocese is supposed to keep of those clergy thought to be possible candidates for bishop, and consulted directly whenever there is a need to appoint a new bishop. Once again, it seems clear that the diocesan synod promoted in the current Code of Canon Law would be a great venue for this kind of involvement. Why does it never happen? Could it be because the clerical culture that holds control in the church today does not see the need for true accountability?

Bibliographical Note

Karl Rahner's account of the "coming of the world church" is contained in his essay "Towards a Fundamental Theological Interpretation of Vatican II," in *Vatican II: The Unfinished Agenda*, edited by Lucien Richard, Daniel Harrington, and John W. O'Malley (Mahwah, N.J.: Paulist Press, 1987), 9-21. Although those committed to a more conservative interpretation of Vatican II do not like it, the best account of the day-to-day drama of the council can be found in *Vat-*

ican Council II (Maryknoll, N.Y.: Orbis Books, 1999), by Xavier Rynne, pseudonym for a very well connected American priest who was in Rome for the council and wrote regularly on its doings for *The New Yorker*. For those who would like more information on the history and theology of democratic impulses in the church, there is *A Democratic Catholic Church: The Reconstruction of Roman Catholicism* (New York: Crossroad, 1992), edited by Eugene C. Bianchi and Rosemary Radford Ruether, an admittedly partisan work which, nevertheless, contains much good scholarship. Finally, the tragic mishandling of liturgical language is well recorded in "Lost in Translation," an article by John Wilkins in the December 2, 2005 issue of *Commonweal* magazine.

Discussion Questions

1. What do you imagine would be the consequences, good or bad, of returning to the ancient church practice in which a pastor/ bishop was expected under normal circumstances to remain for life with the parish/diocese to which he had been elected?
2. If the bishop were to call a diocesan synod tomorrow, what procedures would you like to see followed for the election or appointment of lay representatives, and what would be the three most pressing agenda items in your diocese?
3. In recent years we have seen minor changes in liturgical practices to re-emphasize the separation of roles of ordained and non-ordained ministers and a number of changes in the language of the liturgy to bring the English text into closer correspondence with the Latin original. How have these been handled in your parish? Have they been easily accepted? How is the parish maintaining the insistence of Vatican II that the liturgy is the work of the whole community, not that of the priest alone?
4. If the pastor in the parish and the bishop in the diocese are not of a mind to incorporate lay voice in decision making in the church, what can be done to change their minds?

Chapter Seven

TEN STEPS TOWARD A
MORE ADULT CHURCH

In the first three chapters we discussed the peculiar problems that arise for wider participation in the church from the fact that current structures provide no formal venue for lay involvement. We can join Voice of the Faithful or Catholics United for the Faith. We can write letters to the local Catholic paper or the local bishop. We can be noisy in church or become a nuisance to the pastor. If we are really lucky, we may belong to a parish community with a good working pastoral or financial council whose members are elected, but even then our status is advisory, however much the pastor may in practice let us have our say. We live, in other words, in a condition of at best benevolent despotism, both locally and as a world church. If we occasionally feel helpless to deal with our own democratic American political system, we at least know that there are structures that provide us with the possibility of change, and we still have a vigorous public marketplace of ideas. At least every four years we have a chance to change our political leaders. But no such structures exist in the church, and the places where we can debate one another openly and freely are hard to find. A democratic society thrives, if it is to thrive, on the free exchange of ideas. An autocratic society thrives on the suppression of free speech in the name of authority's version of "peace and security." Which of the two, do you think, is closer to our present situation in the Catholic world?

It is precisely because the avenues through which real structural change can be sought are so few and so difficult to find that it is imperative that we begin to think now about actual practical steps that can be taken to effect change. They may be matters on which we can take action despite the ecclesiastical roadblocks we face. They may be concerns that need to be expressed in the teeth of opposition, despite the near certainty that they will fail in the short term. In all cases they should be selected for theological reasons rather than ideological reasons. That is, they must reflect the vision of the gospel, not merely the political preferences of the individual or group that advocates them. They need to be faithful to the witness of our Christian history. They need to reflect genuine discipleship of Christ. And, perhaps above all, they need to show a commitment to a Trinitarian rather than a hierarchical outlook on life. Then and only then will they stand beyond sniping attacks from those who despise history, those whose Jesus Christ is busier judging than loving, and those whose God resembles an ancient despot more than a loving Trinity of persons.

There are thousands of proposals we could make for working toward a more open and accountable church, but here we will look at ten that may be among the more important or urgent issues to be attended to right now. Some will be easier than others. Some require only that the church take seriously what it has always possessed. Some will take a measure of flexibility and openness to new ideas. Some may even look for radical change.

1. The whole church needs to make an option for the poor and marginalized.

Any suggestions about the restructuring of the church must take account of what the church is actually *for*. The Second Vatican Council made very clear what has always been the case, namely, that the church exists for the sake of the world, not for itself. The church, in other words, is constituted as a missionary community. What we have come to see in more recent times is that this missionary reality is not exhausted in the preaching of the gospel in the narrow sense, though that can never be sidelined. In fact, mission is much more likely to be an engagement with what theology knows as "preparation for the gospel," that is, the struggle to make the world and human life better able to hear the saving word of God. Christian mission, then, is a process of struggle for human flourishing and for the good of the world that God made. This will always mean struggle against those forces that are the enemy of human flourishing. Identifying these forces at any particular moment in history will not be easy, but a principle derived from God's actions on behalf of Israel and Jesus' concrete choices is central to the act of discernment that we need to be constantly making and remaking. In all that we do, then, the needs of the poor, the oppressed, and the powerless must be preferred over the needs of all others.

The option for the poor has to be a responsibility of both the universal and the local church. Catholic social teaching has certainly proclaimed this option on behalf of the universal church. One thinks too of the 1971 Roman Synod of Bishops, which declared that "action on behalf of justice" is "a constitutive dimension of the preaching of the gospel." But it is sometimes more difficult for us to put the option into practice in our local community than it is to hear it proclaimed by the pope. Every parish community has to ask itself if all of its decisions are subjected to this principle. Does what we choose to prioritize in our parish community always put the needs of the poor and defenseless first? Examples might include how scholarship funding is handled for those parishes with their own schools, whether the poor of the parish (if there are any, and there usually are) are adequately represented on parish committees, whether the community has a food pantry or a clothing source for the poor of the area, whether it is a community that is welcoming to those in need. The community also needs to ask itself how to become more aware of the structural issues surrounding poverty. We need not only to meet urgent short-term needs but also to go beyond them and strive to address and change the social structures that cause poverty and often keep people poor.

The option for the poor does not remove the need for debates about public policy, but it gives definition and context to the ways in which those debates should be conducted. Nor does it answer all the questions we might have about how the church can best be struc-tured to exercise its mission to the world more effectively. But it places questions of structure in context. All the changes that we might want or feel we need to make in the church have to be sub-jected to one test: how does this proposed course of action facilitate the mission of the church to be the loving presence of God in the world, given that this will always be expressed preferentially toward the poor and powerless? Aside from the crucial importance of the preferential option itself, it also reminds us of the important princi-ple that structure serves mission. Mission does not serve structure. The tail cannot be allowed to wag the dog, but much in our church today is exactly that, a whole lot of wagging the dog. We lay people need to help our clerical brothers in the apparently hard task of discerning which is the dog, which is the tail, and what should be wagging what.

2. *The lay/clerical relationship needs to move from one of child/parent to one of equality. Adult behavior among the laity is non-negotiable. Acceptance of the laity as equally adult is nonnegotiable for bishops and clergy.*

We have already said a lot about this particular issue. For his-torical and structural reasons, some of them entirely understandable, for most of our history, laypeople have been treated, in effect, as the children of the clergy. We certainly should not imagine that in cen-turies past a learned clergy took care of an unlettered laity. For many centuries most clergy were deplorably ignorant and not much better educated than the people they served. But today in the United States it is simply not the case that the clergy are better educated than the laity. We hope that those with a true vocation to ordained ministry have gifts of preaching and community leadership. If not, they prob-ably don't have true vocations. But this does not confer on them financial acumen, organizational skills, or political savvy. They are leaders of a community of faith. Good leaders harness and learn from the accumulated wisdom of the group.

This having been said, the more important point to stress is that the responsibility for an adult laity rests firmly on the shoulders of the laity, not the clergy. There are several reasons for this, not least that history shows precious few examples of situations where elites who hold a monopoly of power willingly surrender it to those who have previously been powerless. While one would hope that this historical truth might find an exception in a community of faith, there are currently no signs that one iota of true responsibility is likely to be passed to the laity. Those who hold the reins of leadership grasp them ever more firmly. Yet it is perfectly obvious in the North American church that much of its vitality is to be found among lay ministers and lay leaders; could it be that it is time to give them their head? Could they do any worse?

The principal reason why it is a lay responsibility to step up to adulthood is the obvious one that adulthood can never be something with which you are endowed by someone else. Adulthood, by definition, is something we each as individuals achieve, or it is not really adulthood. Adulthood, in the church as in life, must be claimed. The difference is that when someone achieves the kind of maturity that we recognize as true adulthood, families and friends find reason to celebrate, whereas adulthood in the church seems to be deplored. Adults think for themselves and play a responsible part in the society and church to which they belong. Maturity involves many things, including a realistic recognition of the limits of our freedoms. But an adult can never accept infantilization.

The hard work of claiming adulthood in the church is, then, an issue for the laity as much as, if not more than, for the clergy. The process by which we can claim the status of adults is not an easy one, seemingly more one of attrition than of genuine evolution, because the ecclesiastical structures within which our faith communities exist reward immaturity, not its opposite. Surely, Christian adults must bend the knee before the truth of the gospel; maturity can be expressed in submission as much as in action. When the minister proclaims the gospel, mature hearts let the Spirit of God move them. When church leaders offer teachings that represent *applications* of the gospel, mature minds analyze the cogency of the argument that connects the gospel to its application. It is simply not adequate to say, as was said by the Vatican's Congregation for the Doctrine of the

Faith in 1990, that we must abide by "the principle which affirms that Magisterial teaching, by virtue of divine assistance, has a validity beyond its argumentation, which may derive at times from a particular theology." While the truths of faith enshrined in the gospel speak directly to the heart, magisterial applications of gospel truth reach the heart through the mind, and through mature minds at that.

3. The laity and the clergy need to become better educated in the history of the Catholic tradition.

We are as a whole woefully ignorant of what the church teaches, of where the church came from, and of the intimate connection between these two realities, theology and history. In part, this is a product of the American distaste for doing anything that makes our heads hurt, and taking steps to address it might have the added advantage that we would acquire a taste for education that would also spill over into informing ourselves better about our social and political responsibilities. But the most important tactical value of being better educated in theology and history is that we would then be considerably better informed than most of the pastors and bishops with whom we are going to have to tangle in the work of rescuing the church. When we get into arguments with church leaders about how foolish it is for us, for example, to be expecting a bigger say for laypeople in choosing bishops, or an expanded role for women in church ministry, how much more empowered we are when we can explain that all we are asking for is a return to ancient practices of the early church.

It is sometimes said that theology is a highly technical subject that nonprofessionals can have difficulty with. The highly technical side of theology can be a challenge even to some theologians, but there is also a sense in which theological reflection is the rightful possession of every Christian. Yes, nonspecialists can be left glassy eyed by investigations of "the act of faith" or questions of the relative clarity of transubstantiation versus transfinalization, or the precise distinction between realized and inaugurated eschatology. But every time a believer hears the gospel and asks herself, "how does this speak to my life, in the here and now," she is engaging in theological reflection. Moreover, this faithful practice need not always or even often be interrupted by the voice of authority saying, "Let me tell you how!"

If theology is often highly technical and thus not for everyone, the same is not true about history. The history of the church is the rightful possession of every member of the community, and responsible members of the community will take the trouble to learn about their history. There are many reasons why this is good practice, but the principal one is that it discourages us from paying too much attention to the way things are right now. "It's always been this way!" is a terrible fallacy. History teaches us that the church is a dynamic reality, always on the move, always engaged in that common historical process of remembering and forgetting. As a body in history, the church is as susceptible as any purely human institution to the accidents of history. It has its saints and its sinners, its heroes and heroines, its criminals and manipulators. All of them together make up the history of the church, and knowledge of how they have played their roles helps us to understand where the church is today. Above all, it helps us distinguish between what is of the essence of our tradition and what, as a product of historical accident, is not.

Patterns of church leadership offer us a good example of the value of history. Regardless of how we feel about patterns of ministry and structures of leadership in the church, it is impossible to make the case that they have always been this way. The pattern of bishops, priests, and deacons that we know today took centuries to develop. Apostles were not bishops. Peter was never bishop of Rome. For many centuries a lot of the clergy were married. Women held leadership roles in the very early Christian community. Only in the ninth century for the first time did the local church choose a bishop of Rome who had previously been a bishop elsewhere. Laypeople had major roles in the selection of their bishops for at least the first five centuries of the church's life. Now, none of these facts—for facts they are—mean in themselves that the way we do things now is wrong, still less that we can or should go back to the practice of the early church in all matters. But this little slice of history teaches us that what has been part of the church's life in the past could be again.

History, then, frees us up to imagine the boundaries of what is possible. Married clergy is possible. A significant role for the local church in the selection of its bishop is possible. Women in leadership roles in the church is possible. Lay theologians as part of the teaching authority of the church is possible. All or none of these things may or may not be desirable. But, with the help of history, we know that they are possible. Above all, we know that they are in no way contrary to what it is to be the church.

Learning about the history of our church is obviously not something that structural oppression prevents us from achieving. All we have to do is pick up a book, right? Well, not quite, because there are good books and not so good books. We need to read responsible scholarship by someone with no axe to grind. We also need to form reading circles in which lay Catholics can study history in cooperation with one another. Clearly, this can be achieved in a parish context, since most priests and bishops would be unlikely to openly discourage the study of our history. But perhaps the organizations that push for change in the church, to the right or the left, might be enlisted to promote a knowledge of the facts. This in itself could reduce the polarization that currently plagues us. For as someone once said, you are entitled to your own opinion, but you are not entitled to your own facts.

4. Seminary and ministerial training should be for ministry in real life.

Leaving aside the question of what should be studied in the course of priestly training, it is clear that the present seminary system needs to be dismantled in favor of genuine academic formation in Catholic institutions of higher education. To some degree, at least for the present, there is good reason for ministry students to live together and perhaps to receive some spiritual formation from diocesan personnel. But since their academic preparation ought to be of the highest possible standard, and ought to be conducted as far as possible in contact with ordinary lay Catholics, courses in theology and in pastoral studies of all kinds ought to be undertaken in the open, so to speak.

The only reasons normally offered against such a procedure in effect mask a suspicion of education alongside lay Catholic students of both sexes, conducted by professors who may be clergy or laity in institutions of higher education not primarily or exclusively devoted to ministerial preparation. It is hard to explain any of these suspicions in an edifying way. The effect on seminarians of lay presence in the classrooms can only be dangerous if those students are not comfortable in the real world, or if the church does not wish to train them in and for that world. The worry about lay professors is that they may not be as "sound" as priests, but there is no evidence to support this. Indeed, the evidence of learned societies such as the Catholic Theological Society of America would suggest that the number of qualified lay female and male theologians now vastly exceeds the number of equivalently qualified clergy. And the worry about colleges and universities must be a fear of a suitably academic approach to the academic component of clergy formation. So what are we afraid of? Are we afraid that seminarians will learn good theology, or will learn about the world in which they must minister, or both? Or are we simply protecting them from the facts, cocooning them in the clerical milieu that many of them hanker for, and that they will promote and defend as "the way it has always been"? Are our seminaries designed to train thinking and caring pastors with at least a little learning, or are they more often organs of formation into clericalism?

5. We need to insist on genuine parish and diocesan pastoral and financial councils that have deliberative as well as consultative roles.

While there are many dramatic gestures that we can and perhaps should make in the service of church renewal, the unglamorous hard slog of fixing the parish is utterly indispensable. And while this might be attempted through a variety of approaches, cajoling the pastor, writing to the bishop, picketing the parish house, writing letters to the press and so on, the correct approach is to begin from Vatican II's encouragement of the formation of pastoral and financial councils at the parochial and diocesan levels. Canon Law requires such financial councils, and good sense and Vatican II encourage pastoral councils, so we are on safe ground in insisting that these things have to exist where they do not, and that they should be enabled to operate effectively where they exist in name only.

If the first thing to insist on is that councils exist, the second is surely to demand that they be created with a substantial voice from "below," not just selected from above. But the bigger challenge by far is to make sure that pastoral councils have serious and sustained input into diocesan and parochial decision making. The problem here is that these councils are not mandated by Canon Law, and that where they are discussed in church teaching they are always referred to as consultative rather than deliberative. If this means that they are created to rubber stamp the wishes of pastor or bishop, they are a tiresome waste of effort, and no right-thinking Catholic should have anything to do with them. Moreover, if their constitution is wholly or mostly in the hands of the pastor or bishop, the chances of their providing even a modicum of sound advice is severely limited, and their credibility with the community, especially in difficult decisions, is seriously compromised. Finally, why are we afraid of a little democracy at the parochial level? What good would we be sacrificing?

6. There must be real and significant lay participation in the processes by which pastors and bishops are selected.

In the church of the first three centuries it would have been inconceivable that a church leader could have been selected without the involvement of the local community. While the deplorable failures of episcopal leadership in the sex-abuse scandal has brought renewed attention to the ways in which bishops are chosen, the issue is larger than this. The fundamental reason for changing the way we select bishops and pastors is that the people of the church are adults and that adults in developed societies expect to have a say in such matters. How that is to happen is certainly open to discussion, and a number of possible models could be employed, from the direct plebiscite to the election of representatives to a selection committee, to advisory boards to the bishop, and so on.

It seems clear that, just as when a parish is facing the choice of a new pastor, the laypeople of a diocese in need of a new leader must be organized and must present clearly their concerns about the type of person who would best meet their needs. However, to whom are these representations to be made? Perhaps to the metropolitan bishop or the national bishops' conference, or even to the Apostolic Nuncio, but in each case these representations may be thrown down the proverbial black hole. Perhaps a better policy is to press right now, when it is long before a new bishop will be needed, for the diocesan structures to be created that will be activated at the appropriate time. As we noted in the previous chapter, a genuine diocesan synod would work very well in this context.

7. There needs to be renewed attention to the sacrament of baptism as the basis for the understanding of all ministry in the church.

We have already discussed the need for the church to become more aware of the teaching of Vatican II on the centrality of baptism, the close connection between baptism and mission, and the common priesthood of all the faithful that follows from the sacrament. That general call relates to the situation in the local parish community.

Because the Catholic Church has a strong theology of orders and a clear and distinct ordained ministry, we can easily overlook the fact that baptism is a call to ministry. All baptized Catholics have the obligation to explore the ways in which we might serve the mission of the church. All the baptized are members of a priestly people. In a certain sense, our priests who are ordained to serve the church are really ordained to facilitate the priestly ministry of all the baptized. And, of course, the ordained are called to ministry twice; in their ordination to diaconate or priesthood, for sure, but also—usually long before—by their baptism.

One of the reasons that this connection between baptism and ministry has been overlooked for so long is that we usually baptize infants. Only later in life will they be active in the mission of the church. We see baptism as a sacrament of initiation into the believing community, and so it is. But this community of believers is charged by God with a mission to the world. Baptism is entry into a missioned community, and just as people who join a rugby club will presumably do so in order to play rugby, so people who join the church do so in order to participate in the mission of the church. The church is not just there for its members; in fact, it is more properly there for what its members can do for those who are not its members. Only when the church as community and individuals accepts this mission, is it really, fully, the church. Without this sense of mission it is primarily an act of communal self-congratulation.

Recognizing that the church is a community of faith with a mission from God can be an important step in revitalizing parish communities. It depends for its effectiveness, however, on getting that message across to the great mass of parishioners. A community with a mission is not one in which a tiny minority shoulders the burden of mission on behalf of a largely passive majority. Sometimes that impression can be left with people if we think of ministry as that conducted by the ordained clergy and by the lay ministers who work with them in the parish setting. But ministry goes far beyond what we usually first think of as lay ministry—education, youth ministry, spiritual formation, and so on within the parish setting. If the church is a missioned community, then ministry is for all of us, and most of that ministry is exercised in the world around us, not within the parish confines.

There are all kinds of ways in which we can try to build ministry in our parishes, but a healthy and long-lasting approach will require at least some grounding in sacramental theology and the theology of the church. You cannot build a culture of ministry simply on an appeal to voluntarism. People have the right to know that their personal call to minister grows out of the nature of the community to which they belong, and into which they have been baptized. So the first step, and in many ways the most difficult, is to communicate to people three key ideas: a richer understanding of baptism than most of us currently possess (including a new awareness of confirmation as the completion of baptism, the making intentional of the baptismal promises); a notion of what it means to be called a priestly people; and a sense of the church as a missioned or missionary community. This needs to be built in a systematic way into the preaching of the community. Some parishes have also experimented with what is called a "Baptism Jubilee," an annual renewal service at which the link between the baptismal promises and the call to ministry could be stressed.

A second important requirement for promoting the baptismal call to ministry is that we not turn it into something more grandiose than it really is. There are two things to stress here. The first is that the lay ministers who work in most of our parishes are not the models for the kind of ministry to which God is calling the majority of the baptized. These lay ministers are at work within the believing community, whereas most ministry is directed beyond the church to the world around us. Indeed, so-called ecclesial lay ministers are probably better thought of as the vanguard of the Holy Spirit, moving the church to reconsider the role of ordination in ministry, than they are as engaging in the specific mission of the laity. And the second point to emphasize is that God calls us to particular ministries primarily in and through the actual talents that God has given us. If I am a fairly short Englishman, there is little likelihood that God has called me to express my Christian convictions through a career as a professional basketball player. If I cannot carry a tune, it is hard to make the case that the Spirit is calling me to music ministry. If I cannot preach or don't have many "people skills," then ordination to diaconate or priesthood most probably is not for me.

If a calling to mission is dependent on identifying one's talents and discerning which of them could most valuably be put at the service of the gospel, then conducting a parish inventory of skills and talents might be a useful step in asserting the practicality of the call to ministry. The results of such a survey would be impressive for the parish community itself; through it, pastor and people would learn what a huge set of resources they have at their command. But it would be at least as important for each individual who participates in the process. It brings ministry down to earth, and it brings each of us face to face with what we can and cannot do. It shows us all that the Holy Spirit can work through a survey. And, what is most important, it causes us to become much more intentional about our posture toward the mission of the church, and reduces the chance that we will—consciously or unconsciously—just leave it to others to take up the work of the church.

All these steps—education, self-awareness, awareness of the work of the Spirit—need to be built into the life of the parish community over a significant period of time, perhaps as long as a year. People do not become intentional about the connection between baptism as a sacrament of initiation and baptism as a call to ministry until and unless they are confronted with it. Done the right way, such a process can reawaken an individual's sense of mission, deepen her or his faith, and—undoubtedly—reanimate the entire community of faith.

8. There needs to be a serious consideration of the implications of the centrality of the Eucharist in Catholic tradition for the life and structure of the church.

Who is taking the Eucharist more seriously? Rome, which recently celebrated the Year of the Eucharist, or the laity, who look around them and find access to the Eucharist to be increasingly difficult? The Vatican liturgical experts who have produced a large volume of "rituals for priestless liturgies" and seem obsessed by who can stand where, who can touch what, and how many bows are deemed essential to devotion, or those who ask why married men or women cannot be admitted to ordination or whether it might not be a good idea to call on laicized priests to return to ministry? Coming up with satisfactory answers may not be the current priority so much as living with the questions themselves, because they indicate where our priorities lie. What is more important, the present restrictions that shore up our current understanding of priesthood or the declining availability of the Eucharist? The actions and failures to act on the part of Rome are only explicable on the conviction that the maintenance of a male celibate priesthood is held to be more important than ease of access to the Eucharist. If this is so, and perhaps it is, then the message is not clear and the teaching is not being "received." As we noted in an earlier chapter, at this point the onus is on the church to examine the effectiveness of its teaching and to try harder.

9. The community of faith needs to become aware of the enormous resource for education and renewal represented by our Catholic colleges and universities, and the colleges and universities need to recognize their responsibilities for helping the church to think.

Since the advent of the sex-abuse scandal, following in the wake of initiatives undertaken first at Boston College, many Catholic institutions of higher education have shown how invaluable they are to the process of renewal that we are undertaking as a church. Many of the schools offer real theological depth to the church, and all of them can be places where laity and clergy alike can gather to think and to exchange views. In particular, given the unfortunate polarization of the Catholic population today between so-called liberals and conservatives, these institutions may be the only places where the sort of public space needed for a free exchange of opinion can be found within the church.

The size and character of the American Catholic theological community is principally a product of the importance of Catholic higher education. Over 720,000 students attend 221 Catholic colleges, all of which have programs of theology or religious studies staffed by faculty with doctoral level qualifications, the majority of whom are Catholic. Most are laypeople, a large minority are women, and as a group they mirror the generally liberal face of American academia at large, though there are many exceptions to this; and there are a very few extremely conservative Catholic schools, most of them quite small. The number of Catholic schools and the complete financial and juridical independence of almost all of them from the institutional church give them the intellectual freedom that they most probably would not enjoy if they were under ecclesiastical supervision. As a consequence, these Catholic schools and their faculties, particularly the theologians among them, are, on occasion, obvious objects of suspicion. Since most of these teachers are laypeople, however, the institutional church's hold over them is minimal.

This kind of independence, when coupled with faithfulness to the tradition and responsible intellectual inquiry, means that the church has a precious resource to help it to engage the world theologically, even when the church is not always ready to do so. In general, theological inquiry has been encouraged by the hierarchical church just so long as it has been the preserve of (mostly clerical) professional theologians, studying and writing in a small number of technical theological journals to which the "ordinary" Catholic was unlikely to have access. But the transformation of the theological community during the last thirty years or so has changed all that. Not only are most of these theologians laypeople and many of them women but attachment to the spirit of Vatican II means that they are not afraid to promote theological inquiry among the wider Catholic public. In regular classes and in the outreach programs to the local church that so many of these schools have made a priority, students are encouraged to know the tradition of the church and to be participants in helping that tradition grow into the future. In this way the sleeping giant of the *sensus fidelium* is awakened, and those to whom theology still means the private preserve of a tiny minority of scholars become alarmed.

The project of building a more adult church, as we have noted several times already, suffers from the absence of formal avenues and structures through which a lay voice can be brought to bear on the institutional church. The Catholic colleges and universities, however, represent something of an exception in this regard. While they are most definitely not formal components of the ecclesiastical establishment, they have power and authority that cannot be ignored; and while they are overwhelmingly respectful of institutional procedures and faithful to the teaching of the church, they are also committed to freedom of inquiry and the free expression of ideas, even when these ideas are not easily reconciled with current Catholic teaching. It is thus not at all surprising that the church makes occasional efforts to curb the schools, either by seeking to require a "mandate" from the local bishop for each Catholic faculty member teaching theology, or by placing this or that individual theologian under suspicion or censure. For the most part, formal censure works only with clerics, which may explain the current enthusiasm for the mandate, expressly designed to bring lay faculty under the same kind of ecclesiastical scrutiny.

The task for Catholics here is clear. Support your institutions of higher education with all the means at your disposal, because with the possible exception of a dwindling number of independent organs of the Catholic press, they are the only institutions with any real power that can support and educate in the vision of the church as an adult and accountable community. To some, this will mean becoming benefactors, but for most it is more likely to be a matter of taking advantage of all that they have to offer. If having an open mind and wanting to learn is a sign of an adult, participating in the educational opportunities being offered is a concrete expression of that adulthood.

10. The life of the church will not be fully renewed until women achieve their rightful positions as fully equally partners with men.

The place of women in the church cannot be ignored, though it is one of the more contested issues between the institution and the people. In the first place, we need to stress that fact. It seems, as far as one can tell from polling and from keeping one's eyes and ears open, that there is a huge gulf—at least in this country—between the official teaching of the church and the attitudes of the laity over questions of the rightful roles of women in the church. Why would there not be? It is largely a reflection of the way in which the clerical class, particularly the episcopal leadership, does not live in the same world as the rest of us. In our world, the glass ceiling is being dismantled. In theirs it is being shored up.

The institutional response to this kind of thinking is to insist that avenues are being opened up for women wherever possible, that is, in all except ordained positions in the church. Since leadership can only be formally exercised at the present time by the ordained, that seems to exclude women from having much of a role in shaping their church. If this is to be so, the laity in general and women in particular need to be enabled to "receive" the teaching. Reception of the teaching on women's exclusion from ordination, for example, is extremely deficient. A majority of laypeople, apparently, have no problems with the idea of ordaining women. Thus, the responsibility lies with the teaching church to recognize that the teaching in its present form is not being received, and consequently to make better efforts to explain, theologically, how it can be that women should be so treated. The institution is at some pains to insist that women's ordination is not a human rights issue. But if it is not, then explain clearly how sound theological arguments exclude women.

What laypeople can do in this case is anything and everything to prefer women over men for all available positions of responsibility in the community of faith. It is up to us to assist the institution to live up to its commitment to promote women to positions of responsibility in all but priestly ministry. If this means that men must take a back seat for a generation or two, so be it. If we could do this then, by stages, the church would change. So, only female altar servers (how bad could that be, there were only male altar servers for a couple of millennia and the church didn't fall apart?). Only women readers and women eucharistic ministers, only women presidents of Catholic colleges and universities, only women as leaders of Catholic learned societies and professional associations. Only women presiding over parish and diocesan financial and pastoral councils. Perhaps, if it were in our power, only women cardinals, because the rule that currently limits the College of Cardinals to the ranks of the ordained could be reversed.

Bibliographical Note

Many of the books mentioned at the end of the previous few chapters could come back into consideration here. In addition, one might want to look at the 1990 document from the Congregation of the Doctrine of the Faith, the "Instruction on the Ecclesial Vocation of the Theologian." For a frank look at the culture of seminaries today it would be hard to beat Donald Cozzens's book, *The Changing Face of the Priesthood* (Collegeville, Minn.: Liturgical Press, 2000) or the more recent text, *Sacred Silence: Denial and the Crisis in the Church* (Collegeville, Minn.: Liturgical Press, 2004). The best brief discussion of the challenges faced by the system of parish pastoral councils is chapter 1 of a new book by Bradford Hinze, *Practices of Dialogue in the Roman Catholic Church* (New York: Continuum, 2006). Books on the Eucharist are legion, but many of them are very technical and most pay no attention to the tension between theologies of the Eucharist and the practical problem of access to the Eucharist. Among the most useful is a short book by Morris Pelzel, *Ecclesiology: The Church as Communion and Mission* (Chicago: Loyola, 2001). When it comes to discussing Catholic colleges and universities, everyone should start with John Paul II's beautiful document *Ex Corde Ecclesiae* (Washington, D.C.: U.S. Catholic Conference, 1996) and then perhaps go on to Michael Buckley's *The Catholic University as Promise and Project: Reflections in a Jesuit Idiom* (Washington, D.C.: Georgetown University Press, 1999) or David O'Brien's work, *From the Heart of the American Church: Catholic Higher Education and American Culture* (Maryknoll, N.Y.: Orbis Books, 1994). It is hard to know where to start on a discussion of the role of women in the church. The official institutional position can be gleaned from the *Letter to the Bishops of the Catholic Church on the Collaboration of Men and Women in the Church and in the World* (Boston: Pauline, 2003), a document of the Vatican's Congregation for the Doctrine of the Faith. A quirky but engaging account from a journalist at the liberal end of the spectrum is Angela Bonavoglia's *Good Catholic Girls: How Women Are Leading the Fight to Change the Church* (New York: Regan Books, 2006). But perhaps the best might be somewhere in the center, where you would find *The Church Women Want* (New York: Herder & Herder, 2002), by the distinguished American theologian Elizabeth Johnson. Finally, the option for the poor can be found in any book about liberation theology, but also and very clearly in Donal Dorr's *Option for the Poor: A Hundred Years of Vatican Social Teaching* (Maryknoll, N.Y.: Orbis Books, 1992), where he considers it in a wider set of contexts.

Discussion Questions

1. Which three of these ten steps do you consider the most important, and why?

2. Which of the steps are least important? Why?
3. What seems to you to be missing from the ten steps that you feel really ought to be there?
4. What would have to change in our parish communities if we really took seriously the preferential option for the poor?

Chapter Eight

THE LAITY, EPISCOPAL LEADERSHIP, AND THE MISSION OF THE CHURCH

In the last chapter we looked at a number of concrete steps we should take in order to help create the adult and accountable church that we long for. The first step suggested, to make an option for the poor and the oppressed, is different from the other nine in one important way. While the other nine proposals have to do with ways to make the church itself function more effectively, the tenth proposal redirects us to think about how a more adult and accountable church should act in the world. We have devoted a lot of pages to stressing how the church is a "missioned community" and how baptism is the basis for the mission. It is time now to begin to answer the question of the precise content of the mission. What ought the direction to be in which an open church in an open society is faithful to the mission entrusted to it by God? What do we do when we are busy fulfilling the mission?

The Worldly Mission of the Laity

This question of the mission of the church is one that we need to consider for a couple of reasons. In the first place, the church is not intended by God as a community that looks inward to its own good order; God *sends* the church; that is, the church is constituted as a community with a mission. The church is not in existence for God's sake or for its own, but for the sake of the world to which it is sent. Second, the mission of the church to the world is principally the responsibility of the laity, not only because they vastly outnumber the ranks of the clergy but also because this is what it is to be a layperson, to be responsible for the mission of the church in the world. Some chapters ago we considered the difficulty of defining a layperson without using a negation—not a priest, not a monk, and so on. Now perhaps we can see our way forward: a layperson is a Christian baptized into mission to the world beyond the church. This and only this was what the fathers of Vatican II meant when they referred to the laity as "secular." In no sense was it intended as an assignment of second-class status or a demeaning of the lay vocation.

When the laity are assigned a mission to the world there is often a sense that they have a lesser role than the ordained, whose job it is directly to serve the community of faith. This is a severe misunderstanding of the relative responsibilities. There is inter-dependence at work here, and neither makes sense without the other. On the one hand, the work of the ordained is to maintain the community of faith and in particular the Eucharistic celebration for the sake of strengthening the faith of the whole community. The ordained are also citizens of the world and should not bury their heads in the ecclesiastical sand and refuse to attend to our wider mission, but their primary role is service to the community of faith. On the other hand, the work of the laity is primarily one of direct mission, whereas that of the ordained is an indirect mission. Of course, some laypeople find themselves working in the church (so-called lay ministers), but the mission of the laity as laity is to the world beyond the church. The laity, in other words, carry out the mission entrusted to the church by God. The ordained as ordained assist in that mission.

As individuals, the laity fulfill their mission in the world by virtue of their baptism, and they are not subject to ecclesiastical oversight. This picture of the relationship between the ordained, the laity, and the mission of the church raises the question of authority in the church in a new way, to which a novel response may be necessary. It is of course the responsibility of the institution to see that laypeople have the spiritual and theological formation to carry out their part of the mission, but they do not derive a mandate for mission from the institutional church. They already have it from God. If they were to form associations of some kind and claim formal status as Catholic lay movements for evangelization, then the institutional church would expect to have some oversight—this is what used to be called "Catholic Action" in the writings of the popes of the mid-twentieth century. But the overwhelming majority of laypeople are called to mission as individuals in the world, and ecclesiastical authority does not come into play.

Church Leadership and Good Teaching

When we look at the church as a missionary body in this way, with the laity in the vanguard of that mission, it causes us to think differently about the role of leadership in the church. There will, of course, always remain a role for church leaders in maintaining good order within the community of faith, and although the bureaucratic zeal of administrators can lead to far too much red tape about who can do what, where and when, we would probably descend into chaos if we didn't have any Canon Law at all. The far more important role of church leaders, however, is that of teaching, which returns us to the questions we have encountered earlier about what makes teaching effective and what conclusions we might need to draw if it seems that teaching is not being heard. No one who thinks seriously about the vocation of the teacher can possibly imagine that it is a matter of telling people what to think, and there seems to be no good reason to imagine that good teaching in the church should be any different from good teaching anywhere else.

If we think about the primary role of church leadership as being good teaching, then there are some clear consequences. No good teacher just "teaches the truth," though all good teachers see their roles as leading their students to understand and thus to come to the truth about this or that. The student is not simply an empty vessel waiting to be filled with the wisdom provided by the one in the know. Moreover, the teacher is not merely a facilitator of the student's self-expression or personal authenticity. There is always something to be taught, both content and process, and the teacher is the teacher because on the whole he or she knows something more about both content and process. The good teacher also knows, however, that there have been more than a few moments when a student has helped the teacher learn too, has produced insights or examples that have helped the teacher see more clearly what exactly is being taught. Learning is always a two-way process, and more often than not what makes it possible for the student to have something to offer the teacher is not a superior knowledge of the content of the discipline but different life experiences.

The formal process of teaching in the Catholic Church is far too often conducted as if it were simply a matter of the communication of content. When it is imagined in this way, then the one who knows enlightens the one who does not know. The teacher is active; the learner is passive. No wonder that little attention is paid to whether or not the lesson has been taught effectively, whether the wisdom has been "received." Such an approach to teaching is uncannily similar to the well-worn caricature of the bad and boring teacher who expects students to write down what he or she says and simply regurgitate it in the exam. Whether a student understands or not is of little import; what matters is that they can repeat the lesson. This is, of course, the method of catechetics, and to imagine that catechetics alone will suffice is as disastrous as its opposite, the belief that there is no content at all to be communicated.

The fundamental problem with the merely catechetical approach to church teaching is that it is a very poor preparation for those who are called to be in the vanguard of the church's mission, and in consequence, the teaching church needs to initiate a radical reappraisal of what is involved in teaching. The laity cannot bring the gospel to the world if they know it only in the manner of rote learning. They in their turn are teachers of the world; and while you can certainly pass an exam in something that you do not understand and plan to forget just as soon as possible, you cannot teach what you do not

understand. Just so long as the church was thought of as bringing sal- /
vation to its members through their faithful membership, rather than
reaching out to the world in faithfulness to its God-given mission, it
was understandable that teaching would be seen as the transmission
of truths to be accepted. But a church with a mission led by the laity
needs to see its teaching wholly differently; now, teaching must
engage the taught, must be "received," and only then can it become
the possession of those who are called to spread the gospel in their
turn.

A second problem, frankly, is that too many of the teachers do
not know enough about what they are teaching. It is no secret that
most ordained clergy pay little or no attention to theology or history
from the day that their seminary training ends, and it is also the case
that bishops are for the most part selected for something other than
the skills of scholarship. There is surely a connection between this
kind of lack of knowledge and the generally poor level of preaching
in Catholic churches. The solution is unlikely to be found by insisting on further education for pastors or only selecting bishops from
among the ranks of academic theologians or scripture scholars.
Theologians are not necessarily the right people to be bishops, any
more than bishops are automatically good theologians. But there is a
great deal to be said for restoring the role of the theologian to the place
of honor that it held in the church until the late Middle Ages. The
teaching authority, or "magisterium," of the church for the best part
of 1,500 years was understood as a collaborative work of bishops and
theologians. In the end, as the consistent teaching of the Catholic
Church insists, the bishops are those who pronounce with authority
upon the faith of the church. But just as you can't make a silk purse of
a pastor out of a sow's ear of a seminarian, but require some appropriate talents to pronounce on the genuineness of a claim to a vocation, so the teaching of the bishops is likely to be as good as the
wisdom *and* scholarship that undergird it. There is a pronounced gap
between the American bishops and the great mass of American theologians, and in this instance this is not a purely American issue, but
colors the whole church. Many American bishops are at least nominally members of the Catholic Theological Society of America.

Among the six hundred or so theologians who attend the annual meeting of this venerable learned society, you can count the bishops on the fingers of one hand. In fact, if you have lost a finger or two in an accident you can still use that hand to count the bishops. And when the bishops meet in the twice-yearly sessions of their national conference, no theologian who is not also a bishop—and there are very few theologian-bishops—is party to their debates.

What we need at this moment in our history but we are not getting is teaching authority that recognizes the extraordinary complexity of persuasive communication of essentials, the importance of respecting a plurality of points of view in those areas where there really is no need for consensus, and—as they say—the wisdom to know the difference. There seem to be some grounds for hope in the tone of Benedict XVI's inaugural encyclical, which reads much more like a teaching document than a set of proclamations, even complete with phrases such as "let me sum up what we have so far covered." It would be wonderful if the American bishops could uncover such a tone, especially if they could marry it to the far more collaborative style of their teaching in the 1980s, when documents on nuclear arms and on the U.S. economy were fashioned in an unprecedently open public process. But at the present we seem a long way from recovering that far healthier approach, not least because the composition of the U.S. bishops' conference today is far different from what it then was.

The Worldly Mission of the Church: The Struggle Against the Anti-Human

One of the major challenges for the church in being faithful to its mission is to figure out how that mission is going to be most effective in a world marked by religious pluralism, on the one hand, and secularism and indifferentism, on the other. The gospel is the prized possession of the Christian churches, celebrated in worship and lived out in the daily practice of believers. Beyond the church, nationally and internationally, we encounter two types of people who need to be approached in quite different ways. The first are the enormous numbers of faithful adherents of religious traditions other than Christianity. In the United States we meet them as significant minorities within a population that at least nominally remains largely Christian. In the world as a whole, particularly in Asia, we encounter them as the dominant, ancient religious traditions alongside which Christianity is often the possession of a small minority of people. The second are the many millions of people, particularly in Europe but also in North America and other parts of the so-called First World, who are marked not so much by hostility to organized religion as by complete lack of interest. Pope Benedict XVI's wish to place this second group first on the agenda of his papacy reveals two important differences between the two groups. First, the secularists, possessing no particular religious identification but often people of significant spiritual depth, may be able to hear the gospel if it is presented to them effectively. Second, the followers of other religious traditions may not only not be so ready to hear the call of Christ but may in fact have less need of it.

Given the complex realities of our world today, evangelization can never mean simply preaching. Standing on a soap box and engaging in those old-time apologetics may conceivably have had its place when the target was the poor Protestant and the aim was to draw him or her back into the fold. But when the very categories of Christianity mean nothing to your hearer, proclaiming them however fearlessly to culturally deaf ears is just not going to cut it. Fortunately, there are some hints in the Catholic tradition about the way evangelization ought to proceed in such a situation.

Evangelization in an indifferent or hostile world must place in the foreground the importance of "preparation for the gospel," the power of witness and the close connection between salvation and humanization. "Preparation for the gospel" is a term that relates to all that we have had to say throughout this book about "reception." When we can recognize a de facto inability or unwillingness to receive the message of the gospel in the form of the Christian story, good pastoral practice does not keep the missionaries banging their heads against the wall. Instead, the question is asked: "What can we do to create the conditions in which people may be able to hear the message?" In essence, this comes down quite quickly to focus on the importance of Christian witness, remembering the words of those early onlookers who proclaimed, "See how those Christians love one another," but perhaps recognizing that the more valuable witness would be the one that produced the exclamation, "See how those Christians love us and our world!" Thus, witness in a world where the gospel cannot be heard directly issues in Christian pastoral practice that stresses concern for a truly human world in which human dignity and care for the earth, our home, are manifest.

There is great sensitivity to this kind of indirect evangelization in the documents of the 34th General Congregation of the Jesuits, which builds on the central Ignatian insight that God is present "in all things." Explaining the importance of dialogue, which the Jesuits define as "a spiritual conversation of equal partners, that opens human beings to the core of their identity," they suggest that God becomes present in the midst of the dialogue. But "the ministry of dialogue is conducted with a sense that God's action is antecedent to ours. We do not plant the seed of his [*sic*] presence, for he has already done that in the culture; he is already bringing it to fruitfulness, embracing all the diversity of creation, and our role is to cooperate with this divine activity." Speaking particularly of dialogue with postmodern secular culture, the documents point out that "the aim of an inculturated evangelization in post-Christian contexts is not to secularize or dilute the Gospel by accommodating it to the horizon of modernity, but to introduce the possibility and reality of God through practical witness and dialogue." The only fruitful way forward is through a "genuine attempt to work from within the shared experience of Christians and unbelievers in a secular and critical culture, built upon respect and friendship."

The need for this kind of indirect evangelization is a particular challenge to the teaching church. Because the teaching church has been far too much taken up with the indoctrination of its members through purely catechetical instruction, it has not provided them with the kind of comfort with their own tradition that enables a flexible approach to mission. It has also failed to see the role of the Spirit

at work in other great world religions and in the hearts of unbelievers. The importance of "practical witness and dialogue" is therefore
not sufficiently spelled out as the principal task of Christian mission.
Most lay Catholics probably have the kind of basic common sense
that enables them to see that goodness and kindness make more
friends than self-righteousness ever did, but they mostly do not know
that there are very sound theological warrants for carrying these
common-sense beliefs into their everyday Christian practice.

In the remaining chapters of the book we will turn to a consideration of how this approach to evangelization should affect our
Catholic practice relative to the contemporary reality of globalization, and relative to our responsibilities to our own American society. Now perhaps as never before, religious people in general and
Catholics in particular are called to a prophetic stance against everything and everyone in our world at war with humanity. Naming and
defeating these enemies of the human race is a complex and
inevitably political challenge. It will mostly be a matter, as the
Hebrew prophets knew so well, of speaking truth to power in an
alliance with the powerless. Nothing could more surely be the vocation of a community called to follow Christ, whose resurrection is
God's empowerment of the powerlessness of the cross. Nothing could
be a better fulfillment of the church's mission to bring the love of God
to the world. Nothing could be a better proclamation of the gospel
in this present moment.

Bibliographical Note

The idea of the secularity of the lay vocation is a difficult one to
grasp, and a very good place to begin is with articles by Zeni Fox,
"Laity, Ministry and Secular Character," and Aurelie Hagstrom, "The
Secular Character of the Vocation and Mission of the Laity," in *Order-
ing the Baptismal Priesthood,* edited by Susan K. Wood (Collegeville,
Minn.: Liturgical Press, 2003). For the history of the idea of the mag-
isterium, or teaching authority of the church, see Richard Gaillardetz,
By What Authority? A Primer on Scripture, the Magisterium, and the

Sense of the Faithful (Collegeville, Minn.: Liturgical Press, 2003), and Francis A. Sullivan, *The Magisterium: Teaching Authority in the Catholic Church* (reprint; Eugene, Ore.: Wipf & Stock, 2002). Benedict XVI's first encyclical, *God Is Love* (Washington, D.C.: U.S. Catholic Conference, 2006), is available in many places, including the Web, starting with www.vatican.va.

Discussion Questions

1. How does it feel to be responsible for the mission of the church? Is the idea acceptable to you that as a layperson you are in the vanguard of the mission, and that the role of the clergy is to support and enable your vocation?
2. How would you respond to someone who said to you that describing Christian mission as "the struggle against the anti-human" was watering down the gospel?

Chapter Nine

CATHOLICS AND AMERICA'S ROLE IN THE WORLD

American political life is too full of crusading metaphors and the imagery of political messianism. On the whole, and in spite of our good intentions, our world today is not being helped by the exercise of American military might and political power. There are a number of reasons for this. The first is that our endemic national ignorance of the wider world means that we are peculiarly ill equipped for identifying the problems and their causes. Typically, we expend enormous energy on trying to solve the wrong problems, or dealing with symptoms (e.g., terrorism) while missing the root causes (e.g., poverty, opposition to materialism). Second, we tend to assess problems and their possible solutions in terms of national self-interest rather than the international common good. Such self-serving and short sightedness, as, for example, in our collective willful blindness to problems of global warming, can only harm everyone in the end. The United States is not a gated community. And third, we are singularly unwilling to put our national house in order, to show that we cherish human dignity, so that we might have some credibility in working on the international scale for the same set of values.

In the last chapter we saw that the face of evangelization today, especially in the wider world, is more likely to be a matter of a consistent struggle against all that is anti-human rather than a focus on preaching the gospel in the narrow sense. Let us be honest: right now there are far more people in the world who could be helped by food, democracy, or health care than would gain any great advantage by being bombarded with Bibles. Fortunately for Catholics, there are many resources within our ethical and spiritual tradition that arm us to be in the forefront of efforts to humanize our world. This task is above all one for the Catholic laity. This is a spiritual rather than a political task, though it is a challenge that has many political implications. But if it is truly the call of God to faithfulness to the mission to be the sacrament of Christ in the world, then we have no choice but to take it up.

The Challenge of Globalization

The most common term used to describe the novel aspects of today's world is "globalization." This term, like so many other big, fuzzy ideas, requires explanation and is open to multiple interpretations. But most of those who use it recognize that it points to one undeniable reality, that cultural and economic and political forces are making the different parts of the world more and more dependent on one another. In this sense, we can say the world is shrinking, and we use terms like "global village" to convey the idea that what we do here today affects the other side of the world tomorrow.

The social changes that are mentioned most often in connection with globalization are the technological revolution, symbolized in the communications technology of the Internet; the emergence of the global economy; and the collapse of the East-versus-West way of looking at the political world, which occurred with the end of the Cold War, and ushered in the far more complex and even chaotic world that we are coming to know today. Huge changes like these are causes for celebration for some, especially those who can make money from them, and matters of deep concern to others. It seems to many that globalization continues the West's love affair with individualism, technology, and the manipulation of the market economy, and does not pay attention to the larger human questions about what this is all for. Is globalization just one more form of Western imperialism, many people ask, merely an aggressive effort to create "one world" in cultural and especially economic terms? Or are there impulses in it that can be turned to human moral good, a commitment to openness to otherness and the celebration of difference, perhaps?

Religion has a place in this debate about the two faces of globalization. Of course, global capitalism and the logic of the markets is a religious worldview to many people, at least if you recognize that your bottom line values are, in a sense, your God. Most of these "gods," as the theologian Paul Tillich famously pointed out, are really false gods, idols of the marketplace. They stop short of true ultimacy, and so people end up worshipping greed or pleasure or success or, more commonly today, the fruits of the free-market economy. But religious worldviews are also very prominent in resistance to this kind of globalization, in the name of that other kind of global awareness. In the end, it is two competing visions of what it is to be a human being that we encounter. Are we individuals united by our common concern for our individual rights and pleasures? Or are we a human community that cherishes difference and otherness? Is our commitment to the enrichment of ourselves or the amelioration of suffering? Are we for humanity or against it?

Religion and Globalization

For at least a couple of centuries, religion has been largely understood by scholars as struggling against the secular modern or postmodern world, and losing the battle. So much for scholars. Lately we have begun to see that religion is actually a resurgent phenomenon and that it is not going away. In fact, as we read our newspapers we may be forgiven for thinking that religion has too great a role in public events, not too little. In the Balkans, in Ireland, in the Middle East, in India, and in the Philippines, to name but a few hotspots, religious identity and local and international conflicts are hopelessly intertwined. So for good or ill, perhaps both, we can safely say that religion remains a constituent of most human lives. Of course, in some circles and in some countries it is definitely on the wane. Western and Central Europe, for example, is perhaps in process of becoming the world's first-ever truly secularized society, though even this may be an overstatement. At the same time, we should be careful to note that the way that the elites in our world think does not always coincide with the ways of seeing the world that characterize more popular points of view. These elites may be challenged by developments at the popular level, which are often built on religious convictions and which represent alternative globalizations to those of the elite. Pakistan or Brazil might be good examples of this bifurcation between a "westernized" and secularized elite, and a population that lives much closer to its religious and ethnic roots. American neoconservative commentators who write about the "culture wars" are making essentially the same point about our own society in the oversimplified ways they juxtapose "the northeastern establishment" and "the heartland."

We can examine some of the issues more closely by taking a look at three examples of the different kinds of roles that religious factors can play in the process of globalization. Each example illustrates the complexity of the relationship between religion and the globalizing world.

Evangelical Protestantism

The first example is the extraordinarily thriving phenomenon of evangelical Protestantism, which stresses personal conversion to Christ and commitment to the authority of Scripture as a more or less infallible and sometimes literally accurate guide. Do not think so much here of the megachurch phenomenon of North America, where affluent Americans go to worship and are fed a mixture of gospel preaching and conservative "family values." Of much more significance is the rise of evangelical religion in many other parts of the world and among other ethnic groups. So, for example, there is an enormous rise of evangelicalism throughout the formerly Catholic stronghold of Latin America; there are numerous Asian immigrant churches in North America that can be described as evangelical, particularly the Korean churches, and sub-Saharan Africa is also a fertile ground for this approach to Christianity. To give one example from Africa, the worldwide Anglican Communion is now increasingly dominated by African churches that are much more evangelical than most Anglican churches, and far more than the Anglican Church has traditionally been. Hence comes much of the furor in the Anglican communion today over the place of gay men and lesbians, or women in general, in the ranks of the Episcopalian ministry.

The alternative globalization of this enormously influential religious family of evangelical Protestantism involves the promotion of an intense work ethic and a highly developed individualistic piety. In this sense, its political standpoint is, in fact, "apolitical." Particularly in its Latin American form, however, evangelicalism has been promoted by conservative religious/political movements from North America. The growth began in the 1980s, when the Reagan administration favored Christian missionaries with a right-wing message as a way of undercutting the Sandinista regime in Nicaragua. So Pat Robertson could be seen preaching the gospel to Contra guerrillas waiting in the jungles of Honduras for a chance to cross the border and destabilize Nicaragua. While the focus of Washington administrations today is more on the Middle East than Latin America, there is still a sense among many that evangelical Protestantism has a bigger influence on politics than is healthy either for the life of faith or the secular republic. American evangelicals may themselves be beginning to realize that God is no closer to being a neoconservative Republican than a tax-and-spend Democrat.

Islam

Islam is a patchwork, not a monolith, of beliefs and practices, and moderate Muslims realize that their own tradition is as much in need of periodic reform as others are. But nearly all Muslims, moderate and fundamentalist, elites and the ordinary people, are united in their distaste for the unthinking individualism and self-centered materialism of the West. Sometimes critics of the West can dismiss too much, and

dispose of technology and democracy along with hedonism and con-
sumerism. But much of the criticism of the West that shows up in the
revival of Islam is on target, especially when it focuses on globalization. From this perspective, Islam is a potential victim of the form of
globalization encapsulated in global capitalism, itself a kind of jug-
gernaut that brings in its wake a whole host of cultural adjustments.
Why, ask Muslims, do the benefits of Western technological know-
how have to be accompanied by the dark side of Western culture? A
fair question, and one that is central to Islam's alternative vision of
globalization. If Islam says that its ultimate objective is that we all be
Muslims, we have to recognize that non-extremists mean by this that
we must all surrender to God (*Islam* means "surrender to God"). If
this means, as it does, that a sense of spiritual purpose would make
our world an altogether better place, who would disagree with this?
Perhaps only the one for whom capital is God.

The Religion of Global Capitalism

In many ways, free-market capitalism is a secular religion. It may
not have any interest in a beyond, in a realm of reality that transcends
the everyday, but it sets out to be a total and totalizing vision of the
world, as much a religion as Marxism was in its heyday. It is marked
by a vision of reality that is fundamentally materialistic, a cult of the
self that is individualistic, and a sense of purpose that, while it is this-
worldly, certainly has a vision of an ideal society as a kind of pleasure
garden of materialist consumption. As the African American scholar
Dwight Hopkins has persuasively argued, preferring the term "globalization," it is like other religions in that it has a god, a faith, a religious leadership, religious institutions, a theological anthropology,
values, theology, and revelation. That it is a religious countervision
is clear from the fairly consistent opposition of most world religions—with the telling exception of evangelical Protestantism—to
its priorities. Religion—whether Christian or Muslim or something
else—challenges the ideology of global capitalism with an alternative
vision of the human. But global capitalism challenges religion, too,

with *its* vision of what it means to be a human being, the values by which we should live, and the god we should serve. It is enormously instructive for us to see that the battle between religious and secular worldviews is not in the end about whether God exists or not, but about what it means to be a human being.

All this suggests that the battle in globalization is not really between democracy and fundamentalism, as our leaders would often have us believe. Fundamentalism can often be used as a club to clout those with whom we do not agree. No, the real conflict will increasingly be between those who see themselves in defense of the human family and the world in which we live and on which we depend, and those who use the world, its resources, and its people, in the service of the creation of wealth. Be careful not to make this into a rejection of the benefits of science and technology. Science and technology are, from a religious perspective, gifts of God delivered through human achievement. The problem is not with the gifts but with the delivery system, which is not even-handed, and the packages in which the gifts are wrapped, which seduce and entice even the poorest into dreams of consumption that can never be fulfilled.

The Catholic Church and Globalization

Catholicism got in early in the move for globalization. All empire is globalization, of course, and the Roman Empire in which Christianity was born was in its time the most successful movement of globalization that the world had ever seen. The first centuries of Christianity showed the young religion as an opponent of empire. It was a highly countercultural movement, a sect that Rome rightly suspected and that was sometimes accused both of atheism and of treason. All this changed in the early fourth century, when Constantine became emperor. Christianity was made respectable and domesticated, and Christendom was born. "Christendom" is the marriage of secular and sacred power in a new empire, one that eventually came to be called the Holy Roman Empire. Here is the horror of globalization in a nutshell. Raw secular power is harnessed to the power over the minds of human beings, in which religion specializes. This was the dark side of the medieval Catholic Church against which the Protestant reformers revolted. But the challenge to Christendom is much older than that. It goes back to the monastic movement that spread in response to the Constantinian revolution. Monks were at first and at their best still are purveyors of an alternative vision that challenges empire.

A second way in which Catholicism and globalization are linked is in mission. Missionary movements are not exclusively Catholic, of course, but the centrality of Catholicism to much of European culture in early modernity meant that imperial expansion and the Catholic Church went hand in hand. Sometimes, especially in the newly discovered Americas, they were hard to separate from each other. While the Protestant Puritans in the north largely thought of the new lands as "promised lands," which God had given them as God gave land to Israel of old, Spain and Portugal in the south were sure that they were on a mission to preach the gospel to all nations and bring the benefits of European civilization and Catholicism to the whole world. Had they not been given the whole world, as a matter of fact, when the pope in the early fifteenth century divided it between them! All Christianity, then, is missionary, but Catholicism was for a long time missionary in cahoots with imperial power.

Fortunately, there is another side to this story. As wrapped up as Catholicism and secular power have so often been, the counter-cultural strain has remained alive within the Catholic Church, even if often underground for long periods. Monasticism was for a long time a site of quiet protest about imperial power. But what about the witness of two sixteenth-century Jesuits, Mateo Ricci and Roberto da Nobili, one in China and the other in India? Both, of course, were committed to spreading the gospel. But Ricci did it by becoming a Mandarin at the imperial court; da Nobili, by donning the robes of a Hindu monk and living a life of meditation. Neither sought to exercise the power that went with empire. Both chose a quiet and long-term path of deep respect for the otherness of the cultures in which they lived so much of their lives. Missionaries today face the question of inculturation. The Christian gospel, for historical reasons, is expressed in the language and categories of Jewish and Greek cultures and has been propagated through the centuries largely by Europeans. How can it be transmuted to other cultures without losing its essence? Indeed, what is its essence? Is Christianity an apple whose European skin can be pared away to reveal the essential, transcultural message beneath, or is it an onion, which you peel and peel and peel until there is nothing left? Is there or is there not a core?

The Catholic Church today is still a bundle of contradictions. In this as in so many other matters, its internal practice and its message to the world are sharply at variance with each other. To many Catholics, Rome is still the voice of empire. On the one hand, some, the more conservative among them, may rejoice in this strong voice in the name of unity, and relish the certainty and security they feel it brings with it. They are not so different from the people who two thousand years ago welcomed Roman imperial authority because of the *Pax Romana*, the Roman peace that brought foreign rule with it. More liberal Catholics, on the other hand, find the centralizing authority of Rome to be troublesome, since it seems to foster both an infantilism and a lack of respect for the difference and otherness that cultural variations should bring to a worldwide family. Today, there is tension between the center and the periphery. "Religion" seems to be on both sides, not only inspiring the Roman vision of a highly centralized church but also motivating the movement for devolution and local autonomy.

Externally, however, Catholicism is in a different place. In fact, the Catholic Church is perhaps the single strongest voice in today's world against the evils of globalization. While this is demonstrated largely in taking up political positions that challenge the priorities of global capitalism, it begins in a Christian religious vision. In the Christian story, God creates human beings in the divine image and likeness, and when through their own free acts they fall away from this high ideal of what it is to be human, God offers them redemption from sin through the gift of Jesus Christ, God's son and the redeemer of the human race. Through the acceptance of the free gift of God's grace in Jesus, human life turns back toward God and toward the realization of the divine purpose in the fulfillment of history that we call the reign of God.

Encased in this myth of Christian history are three separate convictions that can be lifted from the story and offered to the wider
community for consideration. The first is that the idea of the human
is not totally open ended. While Christians speak the language of
"being made in the image and likeness of God," their claim is that
there is such a thing as "human nature," and that therefore the church
needs to be involved in the dynamic movement toward a richer
understanding of what it is to be human, and in pointing out that
there are limits to what can be considered to be legitimately human.
The second, which Christian theologians might call the dialectic of
sin and grace, understands evil to be rooted in misdirected will, so
that we turn away from our human potential to actualize more self-
centered goals. And the third, which Christians call the reign of God,
is an affirmation that we have not reached the end of history, that is
there is still room for change, for progress, for both dreaming of and
working for a world that celebrates the potential of all its inhabitants,
human and non-human alike. These three convictions taken together
suggest that we are not entirely self-determining, that we are both
free and responsible, and that hope rather than despair should be our
message to the world.

While the Jewish creation story has been taken over into the
Christian narrative and often distorted to justify depredation of the
earth's resources and peoples, at root it is a call to responsible stew-
ardship. As the atheist Friedrich Nietzsche put it so well, "be faithful
to the earth." Human beings belong in the world and are at home in
it. Though Christianity asserts that there is a transcendent dimension to the human, that we are more than merely earthly, this can
never be used to instrumentalize the world. Our ultimate destiny, in
the Christian vision of things, cannot be at odds with caring for and
loving the world that "God so loved. . . ." Catholicism stresses this
view of creation more than other branches of Christianity. The world
is both good in its own right and an icon of the divine. Consequently,
human beings are charged with two related responsibilities: presiding over the processes of history, ensuring that they conform to the
human and that they never turn against us, on the one hand, and, on
the other, protecting the natural order, without which history would

have no place. We certainly have not discharged this responsibility to history or nature very well, but the fact that we must plead guilty to negligence only attests to our sense that the obligation is binding.

While it would be foolish of us to pretend that globalization is something we can easily control, we have to think of it as a human phenomenon. Human beings cannot afford to consider that anything so important stands outside the dynamism of freedom and responsibility, which would put it beyond our control. This is a human world. All human creations exist to serve the human. The reverse of this is the root of totalitarianism. And so we are brought into confrontation with the logic of the markets and the inevitability of globalization, not in a naively negative or dismissive way but resolutely challenging the former to demonstrate how it serves free and responsible human beings, and inquiring into the latter's support for all that is truly human. As we face the phenomenon of globalization, possessed of a religious inspiration, we are simply defending the human world.

Central to the Catholic vision of the human is the belief that we are as much members of a community as we are individuals. We become individuals through relationships, and we never lose the priority of the communal over the individual. For this reason, if for no other, we cannot simply reject globalization, if such a thing were possible. The positive face of globalization is a structure through which our concern for one another and for the common good can be realized. Because the freedom and responsibility that we cherish in our tradition must be directed toward the common good and cannot be a simple exercise in self-assertion, the logic of the markets has more work to do to persuade us that it is beneficial than simply to show that it is a successful engine of the creation of wealth. We also have to see how it can be controlled by the human. Political structures need to be able to exercise a policing action over those tools of society whose very power and success threaten their uncoupling from the human community they exist to serve.

If the Catholic Church challenges the darker face of globalization and rejects its characterization as inevitable or self-evidential, there is a corresponding demand that the more positive side of globalization makes upon us. The logic of globalization is the solidarity of the human family. While Catholic social ethics during the last half century has come more and more to stress the importance of human solidarity, it is only honest to admit that Catholic institutions have not always heard this teaching. Globalization forces us to ask ourselves where we stand, both toward the anti-human elements within global capitalism and with respect to those who are different from us ethnically, religiously, and socioeconomically. Precisely because there is such convergence between what we understand to be the human and how the world is imploding, we must approach our globalized world as both teacher and learner. Respect for the otherness of the other requires that we speak out and certainly that we look closely. But above all it insists that we listen.

The other face of globalization reminds us that we are indeed our brother's and sister's keepers. It is in looking these others in the face, and having them look back into ours, that we find ourselves able to go beyond self-concern toward concern for the whole or concern for the very concrete other. In the globalized world, we are much more fully and quickly aware of the consequences of our action and inaction upon the whole, both for good and ill. Perhaps we can see more immediately today that self-centeredness is reprehensible and that concern for others is more morally laudable. This development in the ways of the world parallels the Catholic conviction that the full human being is a man or woman for others, and that salvation lies in dying to self. We are required, in other words, to look at the consequences of our actions for the common good, not just for our own. The future remains to be made, and human beings and their choices will make it, for good or ill. The present moment is not definitive or inevitable; it is simply the stuff of human choice and the stuff out of which the future will be made. This is humanism. It is not purely secular or purely religious, though it is quite compatible with either. Humanism is a belief in the future of humankind and a conviction that the future lies in human hands. If the Catholic tradition insists that in the last analysis God decides, then what God does, even what God can do, is hostage to the moral courage of the human race. This is the divine self-limitation, the *kenosis* or self-emptying of God. Or, in the fine words of the great, late Lutheran theologian, Dorothee

Soelle, "the only eyes God has are our eyes, the only ears God has are our ears, the only hands God has are our hands." Which is to say in different words the perhaps more familiar little mantra, "pray as if everything depends on God but act as if everything depends on you." And so we are called in our church to become social and political activists, in the name of a conception of the human being and human solidarity that our present world is in danger of forgetting. Politics, in this sense, can be seen as an inevitable consequence of taking Christian mission seriously, not "politics" in the sense of party identification, but in the more fundamental call to participation in fashioning the common good.

Bibliographical Note

The essay by Dwight Hopkins, "The Religion of Globalization," can be found in *Religions/Globalizations: Theories and Cases*, edited by Dwight Hopkins et al. (Durham, N.C.: Duke University Press, 2001). Jim Wallis's book, *The Soul of Politics*, is a wonderfully accessible introduction to all the issues in this chapter, especially his chapter called "I Shop, Therefore I Am: *Wounded Hearts, Wounded Earth*" (New York: New Press, 1994). You can find a fine discussion of the issues surrounding globalization, seen from a Catholic perspective, in Michael Czerny's keynote address to a conference on globalization at Santa Clara University in 2002. Go to http://www.scu.edu/ignatian center/bannan/, and follow the link to the globalization conference. Finally, if you are intrigued about the more theological points, you can find a fuller discussion of them in Paul Lakeland, *The Liberation of the Laity: In Search of an Accountable Church* (New York: Continuum, 2003), especially in chapter 7.

Questions for Discussion

1. We are often told not to mix religion and politics. Is this really good advice? If we do not take the advice, what is it going to mean for our religion and our politics?

2. If you had to draw up a list of the forces at work in our world today that most threaten people's chances to live lives of dignity that are rich and fulfilling, which would be the first three you would identify? How can religion begin to offer resistance to these forces?

3. The notion of the common good means in the end that the wishes and concerns of the wealthy will be displaced by the needs of the poor and powerless. This will require personal conversion. Where do the resources for such a profound shift come from?

4. How does your local church act to defeat the negative impact of globalization?

Chapter Ten

CATHOLICS AND AMERICAN CULTURE

One of the particular disappointments of the present moment in American Catholicism is that the church has lost a lot of its moral force within the secular culture. People usually put this down to the impact of the sex-abuse scandal on the credibility of priests and bishops, and unfortunately there is a lot of truth here. But an important secondary consideration is the failure of the teaching church to present Catholic belief in a credible and consistent manner that shows compassion and recognizes the complexity of many of the moral issues with which we struggle today. If people of good will in large numbers cannot "receive" the teaching, then either it is being ineffectively presented or it is erroneous teaching. This is especially true for teaching within the church directed to Catholics, but it applies too in a different way in which the church makes an effort to influence our American culture.

Catholic and American: Overcoming Dualism

The difficult task of being a Catholic in the United States today is made even more challenging by the American penchant for division and conquest. It is as if the constitutional separation of powers has somehow infiltrated the American soul, so that we live simultaneously in two worlds without need or means to bring them together into a whole life. This is a kind of thinking that infects our political life as well as our cultural mores, and to which Catholics are seemingly as susceptible as other Americans. On the world stage we continue to see ourselves as good people engaged in the defense of freedom, but the world increasingly sees us as the evil empire. To opt for one explanation rather than the other is to miss something important. To recognize that good and evil may be closely intertwined with each other may be a first step in a more adult wisdom about the responsibilities of the powerful. As a nation we are apparently not there yet. Perhaps it has something to do with our relative youth among the "developed" nations of the world. But as a Catholic people within the nation we can and ought to have the capability to bring religious resources to bear on the problem.

The heresy of Manichaeism—for such it is—looks at the world dualistically. In every situation, two principles are at work, one with which we agree (good, the light, of God) and one with which we cannot concur (evil, the dark, of the devil). As a cultural habit, it is in the curious position of both demonizing the other in an outburst of triumphalistic bravado ("let's kick some butt!") while simultaneously exhibiting lack of faith in the good to triumph over evil through the power of good itself. If good is to win out, it seems, it can only be by employing the weapons of the enemy more effectively than the enemy itself. History has shown time and time again that this way we may "win," but only at the price of becoming the enemy we hate. What was Hiroshima if not the ultimate act of pure destruction? What was the firebombing of Dresden if not a more perfect *Blitzkrieg*?

In the ancient world the church rejected the option of Manichaeism because it recognized that the gospel proclaimed the coming of a kingdom that was not of this world, one, rather, that imagined the ingathering of all people into the community of salvation. Whether the kingdom was in this world or beyond it, the reign of God was one that systematically subverted the values of this world. Where the world says "us versus them," Jesus said "love your enemies, do good to those who hate you." When secular wisdom advises "looking out for number one," the gospel promotes death to self. "Don't let them push you around" is countered by "turn the other cheek." The logic of acting in our "national interest" loses out to the logic of the Good Samaritan. Confrontation gives way to the loving embrace.

One thing that can honestly be said for church teaching is that it has tried to promote a holistic vision of life. It has not succeeded for at least two reasons. Its ethics of domesticity and sexuality have not persuaded good Catholics that it offers a livable shape of life. And its social and political ethics have been unable to overcome the endemic materialism of American civil society. The result of this dichotomy is particularly odd. In any Catholic community that is middle class or above—and that means most parishes outside the inner cities—we see the spectacle of well-educated married people struggling to live ethically responsible lives with and for their partners and children, even though this may mean turning their backs on much church teaching on sexuality. These same good people, however, share their culture's preoccupation with comfort, affluence, and individualism, once again often ignoring the church's teachings on war, poverty, global capitalism, capital punishment, and so on. Private responsibility and public irresponsibility seem to be the order of the day. There are those, of course, who would say that what is consistent here is the failure to follow church teaching, and that coming into line on both personal and social ethics would solve the problems. It cannot be that easy, however. It is the experience of good, praying Catholics that tells them that the church's teaching on birth control is inadequate, that injunctions against premarital sexual activity, or same-sex unions, or single-sex couples adopting children, or artificial insemination for childless couples are simply way off the mark, however well intentioned and abstractly "true" they may be. And the experience of prayerful people is an important component in discerning right and wrong, perhaps more important than deductive or the "top–down" insistence on more abstract and universal solutions to what will always be practical, individual moral dilemmas.

One of the principal problems with the public ethical stand-points of the magisterium is that they seem so often to suffer from a vacuum of compassion. A great twentieth-century theologian whom we have already encountered in an earlier chapter, Yves Congar, tried to deal with this problem by distinguishing between the teaching office and what he called the "principle of consent," which he took to be the particular responsibility of the laity. The whole church, overwhelmingly lay, has a role relative to the teaching office, and that is to show by its living witness that it consents or does not consent to what the church teaches. While Congar never argued that the church might be uttering error, he did think that the abstract truths they might be presenting, if not consented to by the whole church, are at least unhelpful and may under some circumstances be suspect. In effect, Congar was pointing to the important truth that consent to teaching comes from the heart more than from the head.

How then did it come to be that a Catholic subculture that in the mid-twentieth century was still quite distinct from its Protestant and secular counterparts could so successfully be coopted into American individualism, materialism, and relativism? Whatever conclusion we come to, it is clear that the world depicted in the stories of J. F. Powers or Mary Gordon or Alice McDermott, or analyzed so sympathetically in the writings of Robert Orsi, was a whole lot more fragile than it seemed in 1960. Indeed, its very fragility invites deeper analysis than simply to proclaim that "the sixties happened." The sixties, of course, did not just "happen." They occurred in the convergence of a number of social currents that mid-century Catholicism, apparently, was powerless to resist.

Often the middle of the last century is seen as a golden age of American Catholicism, but if this were true, why did it collapse so suddenly? The seminaries might have been full and every parochial school surely had its team of nuns, but something was wrong. Whatever credibility we grant to the diagnoses of conservatives like George Weigel or Richard John Neuhaus that Catholicism succumbed to the liberal onslaught of materialism, hedonism, relativism, and so on, we still have to explain why the collapse was so sudden and so complete. Was the subculture really such a house of cards? What was it at work under the surface that assured its capitulation to modernity, for all the vigor and vitality that Catholic parochial life seemed to exhibit?

The Catholic Church of the 1950s in the United States looked magnificent, but there was serious trouble brewing under the surface. Complacency was setting in. If the American dream was becoming more attainable in the new middle-class affluence of the '50s, it was a purely materialistic vision. Its attainment required keeping state and church well apart from each other. The still immigrant church of the early twentieth century has rightly been described as a Catholic ghetto, but one good thing about a ghetto is that it lives on vigilance. Suspicion of the world beyond the community is not an unreservedly good thing, but the part of watchfulness that goes by the name of discernment certainly is. The ghetto is altogether too discriminating, but when the ghetto comes to an end (hurrah!) the capacity to filter the messages from the rest of the planet often goes out the window.

The Second Vatican Council's Pastoral Constitution on the Church in the Modern World (*Gaudium et Spes*) was an effort to discern and correct the drift into moral anonymity. Criticisms of the council in general and of this document in particular often focus on its supposedly overoptimistic assessment of mid-twentieth-century modernity and its purportedly liberal myopia about the world. However that may be, and it may be partially true, the greater significance of *Gaudium et Spes* lies in its efforts to marry the wisdom of this world and that of the gospel. The new papacy of John XXIII that had brought the council into being was one of a man of simple and traditional piety who did not treat the world as an object of suspicion. With his diplomatic background in Turkey, Bulgaria, and France, he experienced many sides of secularity. The vision of a teaching *and* learning church presented in *Gaudium et Spes,* one that speaks to the secular world *and* listens too, flows from the sensibility of John XXIII and from the tone he set for the council. The message of the document is that we cannot live in two worlds. The one world in which we have to live, at once secular and faithful, is one of enormous possibility for the future of the planet.

In two months of hurried debate in the fall of 1965, the two thousand or so bishops gathered in St. Peter's for the final session of Vatican II transformed the official church's relationship to culture. You can see this in a number of places, for example, in the Declaration on Religious Freedom, written mostly by the American Jesuit John Courtney Murray, which simply contradicted the church's previous position that separation of church and state was the work of the devil and that freedom of religion was something to fight against. *Time* magazine thought this was so significant that they put Murray's picture on the cover! But significant as that was, the most significant of all the bishops' statements can be found in their final major document, the Pastoral Constitution on the Church in the Modern World, or *Gaudium et Spes*, as it is usually known by the first three words of the Vatican text. It is, in fact, the opening sentence of that document that sounds a new note in the church's relationship to the world: "The joys and hopes, the griefs and anxieties of the men of this age, especially those who are poor or in any way afflicted, these are the joys and hopes, the griefs and anxieties of the followers of Christ." Starting from here, *Gaudium et Spes* elaborates a whole understanding of the church as having a responsibility to the entire world beyond the church, and—quite breathtakingly—as needing in humility to recognize that it has much to learn from that world. Vatican II thus put the Catholic Church in dialogue with secular culture.

The Question of Culture

In this chapter "culture" is obviously a key word, so we should be clear what we mean by it. We are, of course, not concerned with the "high" culture of ballet and opera and literature and poetry, nor of the so-called popular culture of the movies and rock music, but, rather, culture in the sense that anthropologists use the term. "Culture" stands for that shared pattern of values and habits and commitments and that way of doing things that is the common possession of a given community. Many of us belong to several cultures of differing levels of importance to us. But in thinking about the interpenetration of religion and culture, the culture we address has to be the common culture of twenty-first-century America, that culture in which we all share, even if we are as culturally distant as the Amish or as disaffected as an old-fashioned hobo. But this has to be qualified. American culture, now more than ever before, is enmeshed and implicated in the process of globalization. Our culture is a dominant force in the emergence of a world culture, for good and ill. All the more reason to be courageous and critical.

The contemporary story of church and culture is a complicated one, perhaps even more difficult than it was only forty years ago. In the first place, there is often little consensus among Christians, or even among Catholics, and it is sometimes said that members of the same congregation do not entirely agree on everything! Of course, difference of opinion on lots of things is a sign of health. The faith community where everyone agrees about everything is stultifying. But lack of unanimity does create problems for talking about how the church should relate to culture. The second complicating factor is closely related to the first. It is quite common to find that the range of opinions on a given issue within Catholicism is about as varied as those to be found in so-called secular culture. In other words, the pluralism of our society is reflected in the pluralism of opinion within our churches—which, perhaps, is only to say that the idea of church and culture as separate entities is false. We are all of us, all the time, members of the church and participants in secular culture. But if this is true, whatever happened to "the fearless proclamation of the gospel"? And the third issue that complicates things is that there are dramatically different views among Christians about the relationship between Christ, Christ's church, and secular culture. To use the words of H. Richard Niebuhr, some see Christ as against culture; some favor a Christian culture. Others think Christ is above culture, or that there is a paradoxical relationship between Christ and culture, or indeed that

Christ came to transform culture. As the Irish Jesuit Michael Paul Gallagher has put it, Christians are sometimes hostile to culture, sometimes naïve about it, and sometimes thoughtful and creative.

Perhaps the biggest problem in getting our attitude to culture right is that culture today means secular and pluralistic culture, whereas in times past it quite often, maybe always, meant culture suffused with the language and sensibilities of the dominant religious tradition. Prerenaissance medieval culture was probably the best example of this, but even as recently as the nineteenth century the proclaimed values of Western cultures were closely connected to Christianity and, to a lesser extent, to Judaism. While Christians are sometimes as materialistic or hedonistic as their secular counterparts, and usually more materialistic or hedonistic than representatives of other world religions, they cannot be so in a manner that is faithful to their religious traditions. So they are either going to be unthinking and ill-informed Christians, which is no sort of Christian to be at all, or they are going to find themselves edged into one or other of the two other camps. Culture will become the enemy or the dialogue partner in a complex dance of interpretation and accommodation.

In our own church we have the phenomenon of "cafeteria Catholicism," namely, the practice that is surely not peculiar to Catholics of treating the teachings of the church as if they were so many items on a buffet table from which one could pick and choose to one's liking. Whether we think this is a good thing or a bad thing (and most in a church with a central teaching authority think it is a tricky thing to defend), everybody does it. It's just that the more conservative make one set of choices and the less conservative another. So one person might be vociferously anti-abortion and equally strongly in favor of capital punishment. Another might favor the struggle against world hunger and be quite opposed to same-sex marriage or even civil unions. A third—and this is very common—will draw a clear separation between the Christian life that is focused on Sunday worship and the workaday world, which, while not exactly immoral, is understood to operate with a wholly different scale of values. One of the most coherent efforts in recent

Catholic thinking to get beyond this attitude is the so-called seamless-garment approach to ethical issues, promoted by the late Cardinal Bernardin of Chicago. This is simply a call for ethical consistency. If you are pro-life on the question of abortion, you had better be pro-life on capital punishment and world hunger and euthanasia and so on. The institutional church manages this consistency fairly well. But the majority of American Catholics claim to be opposed to abortion, if not necessarily to Roe v. Wade, while being overwhelmingly in favor of capital punishment, in direct disregard of their bishops and in contravention of the seamless-garment argument.

How, then, can we proceed to talk programmatically about the church and culture? The reality is complex and confusing. The differences between churches, or between groups of liberals and conservatives, are partially a matter of theology, partly a product of temperamental or ideological responses to cultural phenomena. In other words, what makes a liberal or a conservative Christian may to some degree be a reflection of theological views on christology, on sin and grace, or on redemption. But to some degree it's just that we are liberal or conservative members of a pluralistic culture. If Baptists are conservative and Presbyterians are liberal, or if there are conservative and liberal Presbyterians, then it stands to reason that it can't simply be Christianity that makes them so. Just so for Catholics; if some vote Republican and some vote Democrat, the teaching of Jesus cannot be moving all of them equally.

Engaging the Culture

If Catholicism is to have an influence on American culture, it is going to have to be on a basis other than that of a united, biblically based program of social reforms or a call to conversion to Christ. The social reforms we identified would probably be reflections of what we as political citizens thought important, and the biblical warrant for these reforms would differ, depending on how literalist our understanding of the Bible was. And while we all agree on conversion to Christ, even those of us who find the word "conversion" to be a little overheated, we wouldn't at all agree on the social implications of that conversion. What we need if the Catholic church is to have an impact on the pluralistic culture of modern American society is something that we can agree on that is not going to turn off those who do not share Christian or even any religious faith. The question is how to engage with a culture that is not of our making, in a constructive fashion, without abandoning the distinctiveness of our faith and our claims.

To decide how to engage the culture, we have to listen not only to the gospel but also to culture. The most novel aspect of the way we inhabit our common culture is that there is a sense today in which culture seems to be at war with the community. Another way to say this is that the decline of a common culture in the face of pluralism and rapid social change has meant that the common culture has moved from being that which shapes and molds us as a people to that which threatens our communal and individual sense of our selves. This may not always be the way we encounter our culture, of course, and the younger generations of the world's more affluent citizens have certainly embraced the technological revolution with an insouciance that we older types find disconcerting, but deep down, many cultural forces seem to be at war with all that is fundamentally human. Viktor Frankl's analysis remains very convincing, that with the decline of the old common culture we have moved into a kind of vacuum in which people typically choose either to do what everyone else does or to do what someone tells them to do. If Frankl is right, then the way forward may require us to find new resources for self-discipline and a sense of communal and personal responsibility. This is where we really begin to talk about the relations between religion and culture. That our culture is no longer Christian is a fact of our pluralistic world and not ultimately critical. But that our culture is in many ways anti-human, this is a call to arms for Christians.

Our starting point for achieving something worthwhile here is to take a long hard look at Christian mission. What is it that Christ sends us to do? Christians usually assume that they are sent to preach the gospel, and so, in a sense, they are. But that does not necessarily mean that the only or even the principal way the gospel is spread is by exhorting people of no beliefs or of other beliefs to accept the message as it is presented in Scripture. While that is certainly one way in which the gospel is spread, it is one that is only uncertainly, even diffidently, accomplished in a world in which we have been taught to respect difference and otherness, and to recognize both human goodness and divine grace in the great world religions other than Christianity. If we are committed to spreading the gospel only in this narrow sense, then if we are people with historical and cultural sensitivity, this form of evangelization is either closed to us or undertaken only with profound unease.

God surely celebrates the lives of faithful Muslims or good Buddhists, and their conversion to Christianity is probably not at the top of the divine agenda, though *our* conversion to Christianity might well be. God expects us all to be faithful to our common humanity. Yes, Christians are supposed to preach the gospel, but more by example than by word. What is important is that God's love is realized in the world, that this message is communicated, and that human transformation from the life of sin to the life of grace is furthered. God works through us, but we sometimes make the mistake of thinking that it is primarily through our words that the gospel is spread, when of course it is our conduct, or actions, that speak most loudly the truths of faith by which we live. Or not, as the case may be. So our lives as individuals, but more particularly the collective face which we Christians show the world, must testify to the love of God for the world and must be oriented toward spreading this love God has for the world. Not talking about it, but spreading it. If talking helps, then so be it. But talk without action is nothing, whereas more action and less talk might accomplish quite a lot. While those of us who are Christian undoubtedly live within the story, it is an entirely different thing to live out the story. Sometimes, that can mean saying very little at all about the story because all our energies are going into living it out.

Christian engagement with the wider culture will give priority to the implications of the doctrines of creation and incarnation rather than to those of salvation or sin and grace, not because the one is more central than the other, but because "preparation for the gospel" benefits from the old adage that you can go in their door, though you want to bring them out through yours. From the doctrine of creation we determine that God loves the world and hence that the world is essentially good, that is, worthy of love, however misguided its human inhabitants may be at times. From the doctrine of incarnation we derive the knowledge of the self-sacrificing depths of the love of God for us, and the comforting and frightening realization that there is no absolute gulf between the human and the divine. If there were, God could not become human and Christ could not lead us back to God. Reflection on these doctrines leads in to an unusually optimistic Christian anthropology, or vision of what it is to be human. What is a human being? A child of God whom God loves unconditionally, whose home is here in the world that God created and knows to be good, and with whom God restored a broken relationship through God's son, Jesus Christ.

As Christians, we find the most perfect expression of God's purposes and of our mission in the world in the language of the gospels. But not everyone is willing or able to hear this particular story. So it is more important to be doing those things in the world that demonstrate our commitment to Christian faith than it is to be up on one soapbox or another proclaiming the story. The doctrines by which we live have implications far beyond Christians. Our belief is that salvation in Christ is the decisive moment in history for all human beings, not just for those who possess Christian faith. God's will expressed through Christ was for the salvation of the whole world, not merely for the salvation of the few who have heard the message directly. So our task as followers of Christ is to be agents of God's purposes for the salvation of the whole world. If we are persuaded that the world is good, then we know that our mission individually and collectively is to make the world a place in which human beings can grow more and more fully into what it is to be human, that is, to make the world a more and more loving place. Because this, after all, is truly what "salvation" means. As created beings, we are not our own explanation, and we are made to be what God wants us to be. That is, we are made to be human, more and more fully realizing the possibilities that lie in the best and richest understanding of what it is to be human. Sin is the failure to be what God wants us to be. And salvation in Jesus Christ breaks us free from sin to be more and more fully human. Not more devout or more ethical, though those are good things too, but fundamentally more and more fully human. Discipleship of Christ is following in the footsteps of the one who, in the Christian view of things, most fully realized what it is to be human. It is this full humanity that the traditional doctrine of Christ's sinlessness exists to protect.

Of course, *we* are not sinless. We may have to act as if everything depends on us, but, as St. Ignatius Loyola was fond of saying, we also have to pray as if everything depends on God. Here we are back almost where we began, with the Pharisee and the publican at prayer. To be aware of a sense of our own finitude and brokenness is the key, because it makes us humble about our motivations and our wisdom, even as it leads us to depend on a God who is the source of a courage far beyond what we could summon up from our own resources. There is a certain kind of claiming to be God's agents that has constantly endangered the world. Extremists of all religious traditions incline toward it, and so, sometimes, do members of this or that administration in Washington. Americans, because of our history, are susceptible to it. This kind of thinking is particularly dangerous when we extend the divine sanction to cover the specific actions or policies dear to us. Let us instead agree on what a truly human world should look like, and let us struggle for that vision, whatever the cost might be to our own individual preferences.

If we now return to the question of the church and culture, we can look at it differently. In a pluralistic world and with a plurality of Christian approaches to the world, there is no way that we can have one relation to culture, that is, one set of gospel values that are smoothly translatable into a whole program of ethical positions derived neatly from Scripture and Christian teaching. Not only does society not have one common position on most ethical issues today, but neither do Christians. But we can surely all agree, Christians and others alike, that the defense and promotion of a true humanity, and of a world that human beings respect as their home, is and always has been the consummate task of all peoples. If so, then here lies our solidarity and our starting point. As Christians, we may engage in the defense of humanity out of a conviction that God demands it of us because of our Christian discipleship. But while our motivations may be somewhat different from our Buddhist or Muslim fellow citizens, the task is remarkably similar; and the more we work together, the more our effort is likely to be successful. Thus, a Christian focus on creation and incarnation leads directly to human solidarity in the God-given task of restoring a fallen world.

To those who find this too political or too secular, it really is not all that far removed from the battle cry of the evangelicals, WWJD, "what would Jesus do?" If any of us were to find ourselves in one of the world's many current trouble spots, we would know that the Christlike act is not to preach but to comfort the dying and to bind up the wounds of the suffering. That is an easy decision. But most of us do not encounter such horrors on a daily basis, and we are insulated in all sorts of ways from most contact with suffering humanity. Does that mean we are freed to get on with the business of life, or—on Sundays—with the business of prayer and worship? Not exactly. WWJD points us also in the same direction of the struggle against everything that would undermine human life. In our cases, although reaching for our checkbooks is both understandable and desirable, God has given us the leisure and the education to step back and ask about the causes of the anti-human forces at work in the world, and the brains to identify them. It remains an open question whether we have the will to make the necessary structural changes that this kind of reflection inevitably demands. It is one thing to feed the hungry. It is another to work to change social policy in ways that will make us less affluent and reduce the entitlement that economic security and education usually entail.

God wills that Christians be the sacramental presence of the love of God for the world, for each and every one of its inhabitants; and through Christ we know that this means a special concern for the poor and the downtrodden. We are faithful to our mission as a Christian community of faith only when we can say that engagement with all those things in the world that militate against a true humanity is in the forefront of our efforts. So when should we speak out? When drugs and violence and terror and torture and human negligence and predatory business practices afflict the human community. When should we not speak out in a world in which more than 20,000 children die each day from preventable causes? Could we ever imagine that God would prefer us to keep silent and get on with our prayers? Why did God send the great Hebrew prophets if not to advise us on just this issue? They all have the same message, but the words of Amos are the ones that always stick in my mind: "I hate, I despise your feasts, I have no time for your solemn assemblies. But let justice flow like waters and righ-teousness like an ever-running stream."

Speaking out would be a wonderful thing, but it is not enough. Fortunately for us, we are Americans. That means that we are citizens of a country that even today still can exercise an important influence to the good. As the consumer of so much of the world's resources and one of the principal engines of global capitalism, we have a large share of responsibility for the problems. But we have a concomitant capacity to help fix these problems, if only we have the will. Right now, we don't have the will, and why that is so is a complex question. The great Protestant theologian of the mid-twentieth century, Reinhold Niebuhr, would blame it on original sin, which he thought showed up in Americans in the particular form of a dangerous inclination to see God's purposes and ours in lock-step. There is a task here for the Christian churches, to lead American culture in a sober examination of the degree to which our nation is indeed on the side of the forces that struggle for a more human world, that is aligned against those forces that seek to destroy or demean or reduce the human potential and human dignity of all the world's citizens. The answer will be complex, and it will neither place all the blame on us nor will it exonerate us. But it might give us an agenda for social and cultural change that will make us feel a little less guilty about our place in the increasingly chaotic national and international community.

Christians can make the greatest contribution to American culture and an impact on world culture by drawing on our spiritual resources to model lives of self-discipline that demonstrate the purity of our intentions. Politics ultimately recognizes only self-interest. To Niebuhr, that is simply original sin. Original sin affects all of us, believers and unbelievers alike, but we can name it and thus be armed to deal with it in ourselves in the first place, and then to name it in the world around us. Prayer is a resource that we can never underestimate, not so much the prayer in which we yearn for an end to suffering in the world, or beg for God's blessings on us or our families or on those who have nothing, but prayer in which we purify our own intentions. The prayer of the publican recommends itself once again.

Christians engage culture constructively when we speak and act in defense of the human, in solidarity with those of other faiths and who share the objective of a more truly human world. But as American Christians, our greatest gift to our culture could be to encourage the national purification of our intentions. And we cannot do this unless we purify our own intentions. We cannot simply draw up a list of issues that Christians must speak on, nor an easy phrase to know what side to take on an issue. We Christians are as divided on these things as is our culture in general. But we could marshal our forces in defense of the human—or against the forces of Satan, which is the same thing—though only if we can grow in the purification of our intentions. That could be our greatest gift to our self-indulgent culture, bent on short-term satisfactions to hide its own sense of emptiness and perhaps its fear of the future and of the unknown.

Bibliographical Note

The holism of the Catholic ethical tradition is appealed to by Cardinal Joseph Bernardin in his 1984 address at St. Louis University, "The Seamless Garment" (http://www.priestsforlife.org/ magisterium/bernardinwade.html). Three good resources for the flavor of mid-twentieth-century American Catholicism are any of the works of Robert Orsi, Peter Manseau's *Vows: The Story of a Priest, a Nun, and Their Son* (New York: Free Press, 2005), and the novels of Alice McDermott. The views of Richard John Neuhaus can be found at length in each monthly issue of his conservative Catholic journal, *First Things*. George Weigel is the most prolix of the many biographers of John Paul II, but a better take on his approach to Catholicism as a whole might be his book on the sex-abuse scandal, *The Courage to Be Catholic* (New York: Basic Books, 2002). The best account of the dramas of Vatican II remains Xavier Rynne's set of dispatches to *The New Yorker*, available in one volume as *Vatican Council II* (Maryknoll, N.Y.: Orbis Books, 1999). H. Richard Niebuhr's christological classic is *Christ and Culture* (New York: Harper, 1956). Finally, Viktor Frankl's ideas can be read in his classic work, *Man's Search for Meaning* (Pocket Books, 1997).

Questions for Discussion

1. How does the "separation of church and state" have an impact on what your parish communities might or might not do to stir up political awareness locally?
2. Should pastors preach about political issues?
3. What are the good points, if any, about the phenomenon of cafeteria Catholicism? Do you think it is possible *not* to be a cafeteria Catholic?
4. Is mission to the wider community a dimension of your parish community's life? If not, why not? If so, how do you accommodate mission with respect for cultural and religious difference?